travelling together

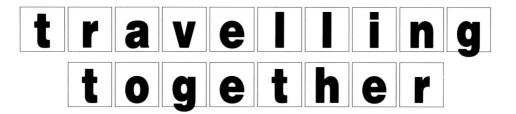

travelling together

Jill Fuller

Collective worship resource for use in primary schools

NATIONAL CHRISTIAN EDUCATION COUNCIL

Other books by Jill Fuller;
Peace (NCEC Project 1992)

Published by:
National Christian Education Council
Robert Denholm House
Nutfield
Redhill RH1 4HW

British Library Cataloguing-in-publication Data:
Fuller, Jill
    Travelling Together: Collective Worship
    for Primary Schools
    I. Title
    268

ISBN 0-7197-0801-X

Typeset by One and A Half Graphics
Printed by Staples Printers, Rochester

CONTENTS

Contents — *continued*

PREFACE

The Education Reform Act 1988 requires that schools shall promote 'the spiritual development of pupils and provide a daily act of collective worship'. What do we as teachers, parents or educationalists want for our children in the area of spiritual development and worship? Moreover is worship possible within the community of a school where the children and staff may well be of varying degrees of faith or of no religious faith at all? How can we devise a resource which it is possible for teachers to use without compromising their own integrity or that of their pupils?

Worship is commonly seen as the preserve of religious groups and those adhering to one of the major world faiths, indeed many of us would find worship impoverished without a belief in a deity and for some of us that is God as revealed in Jesus Christ. Nonetheless at its heart the centre of worship can be an opportunity to recognize and celebrate the common humanity of us all. The spiritual quest is not confined to those of a religious faith but should be available to any who choose to explore that path. It is an inheritance and a birthright.

There is a deep longing amongst many people for the chance to set aside daily activities and preoccupations and to seek a stillness within which to focus mind and thought. Worship could provide such an opportunity. A time to develop or renew a sense of thanksgiving and wonder; a space to acknowledge and confront shortcomings with humility, streaked through with hope and a sense of humour; a quietness in which to bring to mind those in the world or closer community in need of compassion, support and action.

This book has been written with sympathy for the complex demands which Primary teachers face and a recognition of the limitations of the time available for preparation. The crucial point to emphasize is that this book is meant as a resource. It is a framework to be adapted to the ethos and needs of your particular school. The slant of the material is, without apology, predominantly Christian but hopefully the themes embrace a wide spectrum of human experience and will encourage staff and children to travel together into worship.

Jill Fuller
1993

ACKNOWLEDGEMENTS

The author and publishers express thanks for permission to use copyright items. Every effort has been made to trace copyright owners but if any rights have been inadvertently overlooked, the necessary correction will gladly be made in subsequent editions.

'Sunbright Daylight' by Cecily Taylor from *New Horizons* reproduced by permission of Stainer and Bell Ltd, London, England.

We are grateful for permission to quote from the following Bible versions:

The Good News Bible © 1976 (American Bible Society, published by Bible Societies/ Collins)

The Holy Bible, Revised Standard Version © 1973 (Division of Christian Education of the National Council of Churches of Christ in the United States of America)

The New English Bible © 1970 (Oxford and Cambridge University Presses)

USING THE BOOK

When you look through this collective worship material you will notice that it has been divided into three parts: **Setting out, Travelling further** and **On the home straight**.

Setting out is designed for use in the first worship period of the week, when hopefully the whole school community might be together. On the few occasions when special equipment or preparation for worship is required this is indicated.

Travelling further contains a collection of ideas from which to choose and an opportunity to link classroom work to the week's worship theme. There are suggestions for dialogue, drama, dance, story, investigation and practical tasks. In some cases the suggestions might fulfil the requirements of your religious education syllabus or the National Curriculum demands of other areas. Some of the ideas could be adapted to classroom worship but the distinction between religious education and worship needs to be remembered.

On the home straight provides a structure for worship at the end of the week, either in individual year-groups, or for the whole school. Here, the children could present their own exploration into the week's worship theme. This could be in the form of a story, poem, dance, drama or art work. Recognizing that it is not always possible to provide a presentation, additional stories have been provided in some cases.

The collective worship for both the beginning and the end of the week follow the same pattern:

- **Gathering** – a time to focus attention on the week's theme.

- **Listening** – a time for stories, poems and presentations to be introduced by the Leader, who can be any member of the school community, or a visiting speaker. Most of the religious stories are drawn from the Bible. Teachers from multi-faith schools may prefer to use similar stories from different sources. Where appropriate it might be helpful to indicate the source; e.g. This story is from the Old Testament of the Bible. It is a story which is important to both Jews and Christians.

- **Music and reflection** – a short time of stillness in which to reflect on some of the ideas presented in the Listening section. This is arguably the core of the worship time. Many children have very few opportunities to experience stillness and silence and the children may need guidance. The class teacher may choose to use this pattern of music and reflection as the basis for classroom worship. Where an exhibition of work is mounted in the Travelling Further section this could form a focus for worship, the teacher setting aside a short while at the beginning or end of each day to introduce music and to encourage reflection on different aspects of the work.

- **Hymn and Prayer** – These have been included but where inappropriate the leader may prefer to use a phrase such as 'a moment of silence during which you may think or pray'. Where Jesus is mentioned in a hymn the leader should tell the children that Jesus is an important figure in the Christian faith.

- **Closing refrain** – each Act of Worship concludes with singing the refrain 'Shalom'.

LIST OF SUGGESTED MUSIC

Many schools will have music resources which are suitable but the following list of tapes contain selections of music which are helpful in promoting an atmosphere of recollection:

Entente Cordiale (Pickwick CIMPC 926)
Echoes of a waterfall (Harp) Susan Drake (Hyperion KA 66038)
The world of the harp. Maria Robles (Decca 433 869 4)
The world of the Spanish Guitar (Decca 433 820 4)
Chopin Nocturnes. Tamas Vasary (Resonance 429 154 4)
Schubert Impromptus. Daniel Barenboim (Deutchegrammaphon 415 849 4)
Elgar Favourites (Chandos MBTD 6544)
Seascapes (Chandos MBTD 6538)
Vaughan Williams (Argo 4212274)
Essential Ballet (Decca 436 658 4)
Meditations for a quiet night (Nimbus NC 7007)
Introduction and Allegro (Virgo 0777 7 59695 42)
Meditation (EMI Classics for pleasure TC CFP 4515)
Canon and Gigue (Teldec Classical Experience 9031 74789 4)

HYMN BOOKS

Hymns have been chosen from the following hymn books and checklists for hymn practice have been included at the beginning of each theme:

Alleluya 77 Songs for thinking people (published by A & C Black)
Apuskiddu (published by A & C Black)
Carol, Gaily Carol (published by A & C Black)
Come and Praise (published by BBC Books)
Come and Sing Some More (published by Scripture Union)
Junior Praise (published by Marshall Pickering)
Mission Praise (published by Marshall Pickering)
Someone's Singing Lord (published by A & C Black)

THE AUTUMN TERM

Introduction

The Autumn term is always a busy one in the primary school. There are fresh demands to be met: children starting school for the first time, other children adjusting to a new classroom and probably a new teacher. Staff, too, may well be meeting new colleagues, implementing fresh timetables or introducing new schemes of work.

The term, therefore, is both exciting and demanding. It covers the period when the natural world turns from mellow Autumn days to the frosts of winter, with the accompanying changes in weather and light. These weeks includes events such as Harvest Festival, Guy Fawkes Night, All Saints, and the Festival of Remembrance.

The climax of the term is always the preparation for Christmas, when the whole school community anticipates the forthcoming celebrations. The making of decorations, school plays, carol concerts and parties are all activities which make the school a living, vibrant community.

The themes for the Autumn Assemblies aim to enable this community to reflect upon, and explore some of these experiences . . .

THEMES FOR THE AUTUMN TERM

Theme 1 Change

Week 1   The experience of change

Week 2   Changes in people

Week 3   Changes in nature

Theme 2 Coming to our senses

Week 1   Listening

Week 2   Looking

Week 3   Touching

Theme 3 Food

Week 1   Food glorious food

Week 2   Who helped to make breakfast?

Week 3   Fair shares

Theme 4 Lights

Week 1   Varieties of lights

Week 2   Lights of the world

Week 3   Celebrations of light

Theme 5 Presents

Week 1   Giving and receiving

Week 2   Surprises

Week 3   What can I give Him?

AUTUMN TERM
Theme 1: Change

Week 1
The experience of change

Week 2
Changes in people

Week 3
Changes in nature

Checklist for Hymn Practice

One more step *(Come and Praise No. 47)*
Praise Him *(Come and Praise No. 40)*

Time is a thing *(Come and Praise No. 104)*
My faith it is an oaken staff *(Come and Praise No. 46)*

Zacchaeus was a very little man *(Junior Praise No. 300)*
Who's that sitting in the sycamore tree? *(Someone's Singing Lord No. 32)*
O Lord all the world belongs to you *(Come and Praise No. 39)*

Look for signs that Summer's done (Someone's Singing Lord No. 54)
Round, round, round *(Come and Praise No. 111)*
To ev'rything turn *(Come and Praise No. 113)*

━━━━━ Aᴜᴛᴜᴍɴ Tᴇʀᴍ ━━━━━

THEME 1: Week 1

THEME FOR THE WEEK
The experience of change

AIM: **To help children discover how change is part of their lives, and to explore some of the feelings associated with change.**

SETTING OUT
Collective worship for the beginning of the week

GATHERING

Welcome the children back to the new school year, and by questions, observations and discussion discover how they have changed since they were last at school before the summer holidays.

- Has anyone grown taller?
- Has anyone lost a tooth?
- Who has changed their hair-style?
- Does anyone have a new baby in their family?

What changes have the children noticed on their return to school?

- Are there any changes in the school buildings?
- Have the classrooms been re-decorated?
- Is there any new equipment, newly marked out netball courts, playgrounds etc?
- Are there any changes in school personnel – new teachers, pupils, non-teaching staff?

What changes will the children meet during this coming week?

- Will they be adjusting to a new teacher?
- Using a different classroom?
- Tackling unfamiliar work?
- Making new friends?
- Maybe some of them are even starting at the school for the first time!

Which changes are they looking forward to?

- Are there any changes which are making them feel anxious or worried?
- Do they anticipate there will be times when they need to ask for help?
- Do they think there will be times when they can give help to others?

▬▬▬▬ Aᴜᴛᴜᴍɴ Tᴇʀᴍ ▬▬▬▬

 LISTENING

Introduce the following story, which can be read aloud, or re-told in your own words.

SAM'S FIRST DAY

Sam woke up early with a peculiar feeling in his stomach. He lay with his eyes closed and tried to identify what the feeling was. Was it a *birthday* feeling? No – it wasn't an exciting feeling like that. Had something dreadful happened yesterday? No – yesterday had been a perfectly happy day. He opened his eyes slowly, and then, as they focused on the chair at the foot of the bed, he remembered.

Over the back of the chair hung a grey woollen jumper and a pair of long grey trousers. Neatly folded on the seat were his underclothes, his shirt, socks and tie. Today was the day Sam started his new school.

Sam sat up. 'There's no need to worry,' Mum had told him. 'I know that you were unhappy when we had to move nearer to Dad's new job, but your new school seems really great! You'll soon get used to the change and begin to make new friends . . .'

Sam swung his legs over the side of the bed. 'No need to worry,' he reassured himself as he sat on the edge. 'It isn't as if it's the first time you've ever been to school! You'll be in Year Five, so you know what it's like. You can deal with it.'

All the same, by the time he had begun to lace up his shoes, Sam found that the nagging doubts were beginning to creep back again. What if he couldn't manage the work? He'd look stupid and the others would laugh at him. What if you had to eat up everything at lunch – even if it made you sick. Suppose no-one spoke to him and he had to stand all by himself in the playground. What if everyone else came in trainers and he was wearing his posh new lace-up shoes? What if . . .

'Sam! Hurry up or you'll be late for your first day at school.' Sam jumped – what if he was late! He bounded down the stairs two at a time and grabbed his bag from the peg. Mum appeared in the hall. 'Give that to me,' she told him as she took the bag from his hand. 'I haven't put your lunch in it yet. Go into the kitchen and eat your cereal – I've got to leave for work at the same time that you go to school, remember.'

Sam's Mum drove him to school before going on to her own job. As she dropped him off on the corner of the road, she leant over and patted his shoulder, an anxious look in her eye.

'Now, you do know where to go to, don't you, Sam? You remember the classroom Mr Dixon showed us when we came to visit?'

Sam nodded, trying to look less nervous than he felt. 'I think so,' he replied.

'See you tonight then,' Mum smiled, closing the door of the car, 'and remember – *don't worry.*'

Sam heaved his bag onto his shoulder. He took a deep breath, turned the corner and walked through the gates of the school . . .

The playground was a whirling mass of running, shouting, laughing children. Sam had never noticed the hullabaloo at his old school – but then, he had been part of it! He slunk towards the edge of the tarmac area and leant against a wall, his arms folded as he watched the noisy scene in front of him. He let his bag slip from his shoulder

AUTUMN TERM

and fall to the ground. Suddenly a bell clanged and the children all began to stream towards the main entrance. Sam followed them. Once inside, he was surprised at how easily he found his new classroom.

Sam's new teacher, who introduced herself to the class as Mrs Fraser, soon had everybody sitting down. 'I'll call the register first,' she announced to the children, 'and then we'll get ourselves sorted out . . .'

It was only when Sam sat quietly listening to the list of names that he suddenly missed his bag. He had left it in the playground! He looked desperately round. Was there any way he could leave the classroom without being noticed? He contemplated sliding off his seat and crawling out on all fours. No – someone was bound to see him. He was such a long way from the door. He would have to leave the bag till play-time – after all, what was actually in it? His new sports kit, all his pens and pencils, his lunch, this week's copy of his favourite football magazine . . .

Sam's imagination went into overdrive. Someone was bound to pinch his football magazine. Even as he sat there, Sam could see the magazine-thief, heavily disguised in a balaclava and carrying a sawn-off shotgun, creeping into the school playground . . . his bag would certainly be stolen, along with everything in it.

'Mrs Fraser!' he suddenly blurted out.

Mrs Fraser glanced up. 'Yes? Oh – you're new, aren't you?' She looked down at the register. 'Yes – Sam Knowles, isn't it?'

Sam blushed furiously. 'Yes, Mrs Fraser.'

'Well,' she smiled, 'what can I do for you?'

'It . . . it's my bag, Miss. I've left it in the playground.' Sam could sense that everyone was looking at him, and he felt the colour rushing into his face.

Mrs Fraser smiled again. 'Is that all? In that case you can go and fetch it now – and pick up some exercise books for me from the staff-room on the way back. You know where the staff-room is, don't you?' she added, as Sam began to stand up. 'It's the red door next to the main entrance. Knock before you go in.' Sam nodded and set off in the direction of the playground.

Wonder of wonders – the school bag was exactly where he had dropped it. He threw it over his shoulder and made for the red door, where a tall, ginger-haired man answered his knocking. 'Mrs Fraser asked me to collect some books for her,' Sam explained. 'She says she left them on the table.'

The tall man glanced behind him into the room. 'Right, here they are,' he said, placing the tall pile into Sam's outstretched arms. 'Oh,' he added as Sam turned to go, 'if you're going in that direction, perhaps you could take Mike to the classroom next door.'

Sam peered behind behind the ginger-haired man to where a small, tear-stained boy was standing, scrubbing his nose with a grimy handkerchief.

'Mike fell over on the way to school,' the man explained. 'Take care of him, will you – I'm sure you can manage that.'

The staff-room door closed as Sam and his small charge set off down the corridor. Mike was still sniffing a little, and rubbing his fists in his eyes. Sam stopped, and looked down at the younger boy sympathetically.

'Now, don't you worry about anything, Mike,' he heard himself begin reassuringly. 'Everything will be all right. You just wait and see . . .'

■ Autumn Term ■

MUSIC AND REFLECTION

Share some of the feelings in the story with the children:

- Why do you think Sam felt nervous of the changes he was going to meet at his new school?
- What made him feel more confident?
- Did anyone help Sam to feel more relaxed?
- How was Sam able to help someone else?
- How can *we* help each other as we begin a new school year?

Introduce the music and encourage the children to think, as they listen, about the changes they will be meeting during the coming week. Help them to reflect on the different ways in which they can make the week happier for themselves – and for those around them.

SONG OR HYMN

Choose one of the following:
One more step *(Come and Praise No. 47)*
Praise him *(Come and Praise No. 40)*
Time is a thing *(Come and Praise No. 104)*

PRAYER

Jesus, you promised to be with us always.
Be with us as we face the changes of a new school year.
Give us courage when we feel nervous or afraid.
Make us cheerful as we tackle new tasks.
Help us to be quick to see when others need our help.
May we be ready to learn and change and grow in your love.

Amen

CLOSING REFRAIN

Shalom *(Come and Praise No. 141)*

AUTUMN TERM

TRAVELLING FURTHER

This section includes ideas for exploring change in greater depth, and gives suggestions for group and class activities.

During the class or year assembly time, try to enlarge on some of the following ideas:

Change is part of everything that is alive;
Change may involve risk, and can be pleasant or unpleasant;
Change can be exciting or daunting.

● We need courage and trust to meet change.
● We need friendship and support to cope with change.
● Christians believe that God has promised to be with us throughout our lives. He remains constant whatever changes we meet.

A change of work: Moses the shepherd becomes the liberator of the Israelites (Exodus 3.10 – 4.18). This story could form the basis of drama work for the last assembly of the week.

Mount a collection of photographs headed 'How we have Changed'. The display should show the children at different stages in their development, from birth to the present day.

Make a collage entitled 'Changing Faces', showing other people at different stages of life – babies, children, teenagers, adults, the elderly etc.

Ask the children to prepare a short talk on 'A Change of interest'. This could be about a new hobby or interest which they feel has changed their life. Discuss beforehand the different toys, games and activities which they enjoyed when they were at certain ages. How much can they remember about their preferences when they were very young? How much have these preferences changed?

Discuss with the children any changes they have particularly welcomed or disliked. Are changes always what they seem at first?

Make two different coloured display areas headed **Changes for Better** and **Changes for Worse**. Ask the children to write a poem or short story about a change *they* have experienced, or feel strongly about, and mount them in the appropriate areas. On the centre line between the two areas, mount any accounts which are inconclusive. These might be changes which seemed a good idea at the time but turned out to be disappointing.

━━━━━━━━━━ **AUTUMN TERM** ━━━━━━━━━━

ON THE HOME STRAIGHT
Collective worship for the end of the week

 ## GATHERING

Remind the children that they have been exploring the theme of change, and ask some of them to describe what they have been making or doing.

 ## LISTENING

If a particular class is responsible for this act of worship arrange for them to show something they have made, read a poem, a piece of written work, or talk about their reflections on changes.

 ## MUSIC AND REFLECTION

Introduce the music and ask the children to think about the happenings of the past week while they listen.

- How have they coped with the changes of the first week of term?
- Which changes have gone well for them?
- Have any changes made them sad or worried?
- Can they make any changes to make things better?

 ## SONG OR HYMN

My faith, it is an oaken staff *(Come and Praise No. 46)*

 ## PRAYER

Lord, thank you for being with us through all the changes of this week. We thank you for those who comforted us when we were nervous or afraid: For those who encouraged us, when we felt we had failed; For those who shared our happiness, when we had done well; For those with whom we have shared laughter and games; May your love, courage and peace surround and bless us always.

Amen

 ## CLOSING REFRAIN

Shalom *(Come and Praise No. 141)*

THEME 1: Week 2

THEME FOR THE WEEK
Changes in people

AIM: To help the children to appreciate how people can change their outlook on life and how it is possible to change the world around them.

SETTING OUT
Collective worship for the beginning of the week

GATHERING

Remind the children that they are thinking about change and have been observing how people cope with changes in life. Explain that during the coming week, they will be looking at how people can change their attitudes and viewpoints and how some people can change the world around them.

- Can they think of times when they had to change their opinions about someone or something? (Someone who used to hate the taste of tomatoes but suddenly discovered they were delicious. Someone who never wore red but then found the colour suited them. Perhaps thinking someone was really mean but then found them to be very generous.)
- Can they think of anyone else who has changed their viewpoint? (St Paul used to persecute Christians and then became a Christian. Someone who used to be a drug addict but then reformed.)
- Can they think of anyone whose actions changed the world around them? (Bob Geldof by raising money for famine stricken Ethiopia. William Wilberforce by abolishing the slave trade. Elizabeth Fry by reforming prisons. Esther Rantzen by establishing Childline.)

━━━━━━━━━━━━━━ **AUTUMN TERM** ━━━━━━━━━━━━━━

 LISTENING

Introduce the following story about a man who changed his whole attitude to life. Explain that the story is set in the Holy Land at the time of Jesus.

A CHANGED MAN

The sun was blazing in the city of Jericho. Around the well the women chatted as they waited to fill their jars with water. They were talking about Zacchaeus, the most unpopular man in the town.

Zacchaeus had the job of collecting taxes. Everyone understood that they had to pay taxes but the trouble was that Zacchaeus was a cheat. Instead of charging the right amount, he charged everyone more and pocketed the extra himself. He was always on the lookout for making a quick profit no matter who suffered.

'Poor Benjamin is so worried,' said Anna, 'Zacchaeus took so much money in taxes Benjamin wonders if he has enough money left to buy food for the family.'

'It's not as if Zacchaeus needs the money,' Elizabeth added, 'you can see how rich he is, with all the profit's he's made over the years. He must be the meanest, unkindest man in town.'

'He's so short. Such a shrimp, perhaps he thinks his money will buy him a few extra centimetres in height,' one of the other women jeered.

Just then Anna's son Peter came running towards them waving his arms and shouting, 'Mum! Mum, guess who's visiting Jericho today? Jesus! You know, the man from Nazareth everyone's talking about. Come quickly, the High street is already crowded. If you don't hurry you won't get a place where you can see him.'

All the women rushed home with their water pots. Anna and Peter hurried to the High street to find the best vantage point to see Jesus. They stood under the shade of a sycamore tree. Suddenly the crowd began to wave and shout, craning their necks to see the band of people at the end of the street. It was Jesus arriving with his followers. Slowly he walked along but just as he drew level with Anna and Peter he stopped. He stood below the sycamore tree and looked up. Then he called out, 'Zacchaeus! Zacchaeus!' Anna, Peter and the rest of the crowd stared in astonishment. There was Zacchaeus hanging to one of the branches of the tree.

'I wanted to see you Lord,' explained Zacchaeus, 'I'm so short, I couldn't see you from the ground, so I climbed into this sycamore tree.'

'Well come down now,' said Jesus, 'I want to have a meal at your house today.'

There was a gasp of amazement from all the by-standers. Jesus was asking to eat at Zacchaeus's house! The people all muttered disapprovingly but Jesus waited patiently as Zacchaeus scrambled down from the tree and led Jesus to his home.

The crowd stood around for some time murmuring their annoyance that Jesus should have chosen to eat with the most unpopular man in town.

The next day, as usual, the women were around the well filling their water jars.

'Have you heard about Zacchaeus?' Sarah asked.

'I've heard, but I can't believe it's true,' said Anna.

'It seems incredible, but it is,' replied Elizabeth, 'Benjamin's wife Mary came to tell me this morning. After Jesus had left Zacchaeus's house last evening, Zacchaeus went

■ AUTUMN TERM ■

straight round to Benjamin and paid him back all the money he had wrongfully charged him. What's more, he paid not once, not twice, not three times but four times the amount he had originally taken'.

'I've heard,' said Anna, 'that he's promised to repay everyone he's ever cheated. Can he really have changed that much?'

'Well, that Jesus must have said something to alter his viewpoint,' said Sarah. 'Zacchaeus is a different man. He's not so greedy. He's really trying to care for his neighbours and be a good friend.

Jesus has turned his world upside down.'

MUSIC AND REFLECTION

Introduce the music and ask the children to reflect on how Zacchaeus changed and how his change of attitude affected those around him.

HYMN

Zacchaeus was a very little man (*Junior Praise No. 300*)
Who's that sitting in the sycamore tree? (*Someone's singing Lord No. 32*)

PRAYER

Let us think how Zacchaeus changed his life after he had met Jesus. Instead of wanting to keep everything for himself Zacchaeus was ready to give things to others. Zacchaeus became a more loving and caring person.

Help us to see how we can change our lives to become more loving to those around us.

Amen

CLOSING REFRAIN

Shalom (*Come and Praise No. 141*)

■ Autumn Term ■

TRAVELLING FURTHER
Through discussion try to draw out and establish:

- That it may be necessary to change attitudes or life style to progress.
- That it is possible to initiate change or progress.
- That change requires hard work and courage and can be painful.

Make a zig-zag book or frieze telling the story of Zacchaeus or act out the story.

Look at stories of other people whose lives were changed by Jesus.
  Blind Bartimaeus (Mark 10.46 – 52).
  The paralysed man (Luke 5.17 – 26).
  St Paul on the road to Damascus (Acts 9.1 – 30).

A change of heart – Discuss with the children times when they have changed their viewpoint about something: rules at home, a particular friendship, something they liked or disliked doing.

A changed person – Help the children to explore their hopes for themselves. How would they like to change? What can they do to make change happen? Can they make a plan of action to help them achieve the changes they hope for?

Ask each child to write the way they want to change on a postcard and complete their plan of action for achieving it:

Changes I would like to make . . . .

To achieve this I must . . . .

My first step is . . . .

ON THE HOME STRAIGHT
Collective worship for the end of the week

 ## GATHERING

Remind the children that they have been exploring changes in people.

 ## LISTENING

Arrange for the class or group responsible to act out a drama, read a story they have written, or share their dreams of changed people or circumstances.

 ## MUSIC AND REFLECTION

Introduce the music and ask the children to think, during the music, about how they can change their lives to make themselves, and those around them, happier.

 ## HYMN

O Lord, all the world belongs to you *(Come and Praise No. 39)*

 ## PRAYER

Lord grant me the serenity to accept the things I cannot change, the courage to change the things I can and the wisdom to know the difference.

Amen

 ## CLOSING REFRAIN

Shalom *(Come and Praise No. 141)*

▬ Autumn Term ▬

THEME 1: Week 3

THEME FOR THE WEEK
Changes in nature

AIM: To awaken childrens' awareness of natural life cycles and rhythms and to be observant of the changes in nature.

 SETTING OUT

Collective worship for the beginning of the week

GATHERING

Remind the children that they have been thinking about change and ask them what changes they have noticed in the world outside the school and the world of nature. The direction of the questions will depend on whether the children can observe nature easily, as in a rural school, or whether the questions must be related to an urban environment.

● What is happening to the trees or the displays in the shop windows? (Leaves changing colour, acorns and conkers forming, autumn and winter clothes displayed in the shop windows.)

● What is happening to the day? (Slightly darker in the mornings and evenings, changes in temperature.)

● What is happening to their choice of food? (Enjoying warmer meals rather than salads, fewer opportunities for picnics or barbecues.)

● What is happening to the games they play or watch on television? (Football and rugby season now well under way, cricket season ended. Are they playing indoor games after school?)

● Explain that as the year changes it moves through four different periods of spring, summer, autumn and winter and that these are called seasons.

■ AUTUMN TERM ■

 LISTENING

Introduce and read the following:

There is a season and a time for everything under heaven.
A time for work and a time for play.
A time for planting seeds and a time for gathering the crops.
A time for sunshine and a time for rain.
A time for the darkness of night and a time for the light of day.
A time for stormy weather and a time for quiet days.
A time to remember and a time to forget.
A time to speak and a time to listen.
Watch for these times and changes so that you may understand the rhythm of life and feel its heartbeat.

(Adapted from Ecclesiastes 3)

 MUSIC AND REFLECTION

Ask the children to listen to the music and to think of all the changes in nature they experience each day.

 HYMN

Look for signs that summer's done *(Someone's singing Lord No. 54)*

 PRAYER

Lord, help us to be aware of the rhythms and changes in the world around us and to see them all as gifts from you.

Sunrise and sunset.
Work and play.
Light and dark.
Laughter and tears.
May we trust that all things come from your love.

Amen

 CLOSING REFRAIN

Shalom *(Come and Praise No. 141)*

■ Autumn Term ■

TRAVELLING FURTHER
Continue the theme of changes in nature

In your class or year worship time try to draw out:

- An awareness of the seasons.
- An appreciation of the rhythms of life: light and dark, day and night, rest and activity, living and dying.
- The fact that changing and moving with the rhythm is a life giving pattern.
- An awareness of the life cycle and changes in all living things.

Make a collage of four panels depicting the four seasons.

Make an anthology of favourite poems about the seasons.

Study the movement of the earth in relation to the sun and discuss how this causes day and night and the pattern of the seasons.

Study the life cycle of a tadpole to a frog, caterpillar to butterfly or the migration patterns of birds.

USEFUL BOOKS:

The four books *Spring, Summer, Autumn, Winter* (published by Wayland).
The Life Cycle Series (includes the life cycle of the butterfly, frog and swallow) (published by Wayland).

ON THE HOME STRAIGHT
Collective worship for the end of the week

GATHERING

Remind the children that they have been exploring the changes around them.

Autumn Term

LISTENING

Arrange for the class responsible to show something they have made or talk about their study. Alternatively show a film strip or video about the changing of the seasons.

USEFUL RESOURCES

Topic Picture Packs slides and filmstrips available from
Philip Green Educational Ltd, 112a Alcester Road, Studley, Warwickshire, B80 7NR Telephone 0527 854711

MUSIC AND REFLECTION

Introduce the music and ask the children to reflect on their favourite season or time of day.

HYMN

Round, round, round *(Come and Praise No. 111)*
To ev'rything, turn *(Come and Praise No. 113)*

PRAYER

Thank you God for the richness of the changing seasons of the year. Help us to enjoy each one and to appreciate all the opportunities each experience brings.

Amen

CLOSING REFRAIN

Shalom *(Come and Praise No. 141)*

AUTUMN TERM
THEME 2: *Coming to our senses*

Week 1
Listening

Week 2
Looking

Week 3
Touching

Checklist for Hymn Practice

I listen and I listen *(Come and Praise No. 60)*
Music of the world a-turning *(Alleluya, 77 songs for thinking people No. 19)*

Give to us eyes that we may truly see *(Someone's singing Lord No. 18)*
He made me *(Come and Praise No. 18)*

Jesus' hands were kind hands *(Someone's singing Lord No. 33)*
Hands to work and feet to run *(Someone's singing Lord No. 21)*

THEME 2: Week 1

THEME FOR THE WEEK
Listening

AIM: **To help the children appreciate the gift of hearing and to be aware of the world of the hearing impaired.**

SETTING OUT
Collective worship for the beginning of the week

 ## GATHERING

Introduce the theme of our senses and explain that this week they will be exploring sounds and hearing.

- What sounds did they hear when they woke up?
- What sounds did they hear as they walked to school?
- Are there sounds they like and dislike?
- What would they miss most if they could not hear at all?
- What sounds can they hear now if everyone is very still?

 ## LISTENING

Introduce the following poem.

FAVOURITE SOUNDS

I like the early morning sounds.
Dad clattering the china in the kitchen.
My brother whistling as he splashes whilst he's shaving.
My sister thumping to the rhythm of the radio.
I like the sounds of early morning.

I like midday sounds.
The scraping of knives and forks across the dishes.
The chatter of friends and dinner ladies calling.
The shouts and screams of games in the playground.
I like the sounds of the middle of the day.

I like evening sounds.
The whistle of the kettle as it sings at supper time.
The mewing of my cat waiting to be fed.
The clicking of the latch-key which heralds Dad's arrival.
I like the sounds of the evening.

I like night-time sounds.
Scraps of conversation from lads passing by our window.
Milk bottles clanking as they're put out on the doorstep.
The quiet of my breathing in the silence of my room.
I like the sounds of night-time.

MUSIC AND REFLECTION

Introduce the music and ask the children to think of all the sounds they enjoy and to give thanks for them.

HYMN

I listen and I listen *(Come and Praise No. 60)*

PRAYER

Teach me to listen Lord:
To listen to the everyday sounds around me.
To listen to the sounds of music and laughter.
To listen to my friends and really hear what they are saying.
To be thankful for the wonderful gift of hearing.

Amen

CLOSING REFRAIN

Shalom *(Come and Praise No. 141)*

TRAVELLING FURTHER

Use some of the following ideas for continuing reflection on the theme of listening.

In your class and year worship time try to:

- Encourage the children to appreciate the variety of sounds.
- Help the children to feel at ease with silence.
- Promote careful and attentive listening.
- Encourage the children to be sympathetic to those with impaired hearing.

Tell the story of Samuel the boy who listened (1 Samuel 3.1 – 10)

Devise a sound quiz. One child stands behind a screen and makes sound effects such as scraping the teeth of a comb, tearing paper, pouring water. Ask the class to guess the sound.

Compose a class poem entitled 'Sounds we enjoy, sounds we dislike'.

Prepare a presentation of sounds, music and poems entitled 'A feast for your ears.'

Teach the class a rhythm or rap poem or musical round which requires listening carefully to each other.

Collect a series of stories, newspaper articles or poems to read to the class. Have ready graded questions about each extract to see how well they listened. Older children might enjoy preparing the extracts and questions for the class themselves.

With the children, find out how the ear works or learn some of the signing language to communicate with those who cannot hear.

■■■ AUTUMN TERM ■■■

ON THE HOME STRAIGHT
Collective worship for the end of the week

 ## GATHERING

Remind the children that they have been considering the gift of hearing and the wonder of sound.

 ## LISTENING

Choose one of the following activities:

- Arrange for a presentation of class work achieved during the 'Travelling Further' sessions.
- Arrange a visit from a member of the Royal National Institute for the Deaf, 105 Gower Street, London W1 Telephone 071 387 0833, to talk about the world of the hearing impaired.
- Arrange for the children to act out the story of Samuel, the boy who listened.
- Arrange for a musician to visit and talk about his instrument.

 ## MUSIC AND REFLECTION

Introduce the music and choose a direction for reflection linked to one of the activities experienced in the Listening section.

 ## HYMN

Music of the world a-turning *(Alleluya, 77 songs for thinking people No. 19)*

 ## PRAYER

We thank you God for the wonderful gift of hearing.
Help us to appreciate all the sounds around us and also to enjoy the beauty of silence. Make us kind and helpful to those who cannot hear and whose lives may be lonely or isolated.

Amen

↖↑↗ CLOSING REFRAIN

Shalom *(Come and Praise No. 141)*

Autumn Term

THEME 2: Week 2

THEME FOR THE WEEK
Looking

AIM: **To help the children appreciate the gift of sight and to be aware of the world of the visually impaired.**

SETTING OUT
Collective worship for the beginning of the week

 ## GATHERING

Introduce the theme of the week explaining that they will be exploring the gift of sight.

● Ask the children which sight they would miss the most if they could not see. (Would it be: the faces of parents or friends, the television, books, a particular view?)
● If they could not see, what tasks would be difficult? (Finding lost items, reading, playing sports, carrying out hobbies?)
● If they could not see, what tasks would be dangerous? (Crossing the road, cooking, using knives and scissors?)
● If they could not see, would anything be impossible?
● If they could not see, how would they find out about the world around them? (Through sounds, through touching?)

 ## LISTENING

Introduce the following:

JEAN'S SONG

I am blind.
Your smile I cannot see.
My fingers trace your face and bring its shape to me.

I am blind.
Your hair I cannot see.
My fingers feel its texture and tell its length to me.

THEME 2: Week 2

AUTUMN TERM

I am blind.
This room I cannot see.
My hands reach out to touch and warn. They are a guide to me.

I am blind.
The colour of this drink I cannot see.
But I can feel its warmth and know the taste it brings to me.

I am blind.
The book you read I cannot see.
But if I touch the words in Braille the meaning comes to me.

Sharp and smooth,
Hot or cold,
Narrow and wide I know.
But what of the colours of the sunset
Or the brilliant white of fresh snow?

 ## MUSIC AND REFLECTION

Introduce the music and ask the children to reflect on what they enjoy seeing.

 ## HYMN

Give to us eyes that we may truly see *(Someone's Singing Lord No. 18)*

 ## PRAYER

We thank you God for the wonderful gift of sight.
Sights which are familiar and welcoming.
Sights which give us pleasure and refreshment.
Sights which warn us of danger and keep us safe.
Distant views of hills and mountains.
Details we can examine close to hand.
Help us to be aware this week of all the things we can do because we can see.

Amen

 ## CLOSING REFRAIN

Shalom *(Come and Praise No. 141)*

AUTUMN TERM

TRAVELLING FURTHER

Use some of the following ideas to continue reflection on the theme of looking.

In your class or year worship time try to:

- Raise the children's appreciation of sight. (Ask them how far can they see? What can they see under a microscope? How many shades of colour can they distinguish?)
- Encourage an appreciation of beauty in art, architecture, craft and nature.
- Help the children to be observant and to look carefully and attentively.
- Develop an awareness and concern for the world of the visually impaired.

Tell or act out the story of Blind Bartimaeus (Mark 10.46 – 52).

With the children make a collection of things which they enjoy looking at. Entitle the exhibition 'Beautiful to look at'. This could include photographs, china, wood carving, collections of flowers, grasses, stones and shells, and reproductions of paintings.

Write, or record on tape, as detailed a description as possible of 'The view from . . .' (the window, the top of the hill).

Paint a picture in one colour only to show a variety of shades.

Using a mirror, or working in pairs, draw a picture of an eye.

Find out about the work of the 'Guide Dogs for the Blind'.

Find out about the story of Braille or the story of Helen Keller.

USEFUL BOOKS AND INFORMATION

Helen Keller by Nina Morgan, from life series (published by Wayland).
Louis Braille by Peggy Burns, from life series (published by Wayland).
Royal National Institute for the Blind, 224 Great Portland Street, London W1 N 6AA Telephone 071 388 1266.
Guide Dogs for the Blind Association, Hillfield, Burghfield Common, Reading, Berkshire RG7 3WG Telephone 0734 835555

ON THE HOME STRAIGHT
Collective worship for the end of the week

GATHERING

Remind the children that they have been thinking about the gift of sight.

LISTENING

Arrange a visiting speaker from the Guide Dogs for the Blind Association. Alternatively a group of children may like to tell the story of Braille or the story of Helen Keller.

MUSIC AND REFLECTION

Introduce the music and choose a direction for reflection linked to experience gained in the Listening section.

HYMN

He made me *(Come and Praise No. 18)*

PRAYER

Invite the children to respond after each line with the words 'We thank you God'.

For the sight of a smile on my friend's face.
For the beauty of trees against a blue sky.
For the wonder of waves crashing against the rocks.
For the splendour of mountains and sunsets
For the excitement of watching a football match.
For the relaxation of playing games and watching television.
For the satisfaction of all we can do because we can see.

Amen

CLOSING REFRAIN

Shalom *(Come and Praise No. 141)*

▬▬▬▬▬▬▬ Aᴜᴛᴜᴍɴ Tᴇʀᴍ ▬▬▬▬▬▬▬

THEME 2: Week 3

THEME FOR THE WEEK
Touching

AIM: **to help the children become more aware of the experience of touch and how it affects them.**

SETTING OUT
Collective worship for the beginning of the week

 ## GATHERING

Remind the children that they have been thinking about their senses and introduce the theme of touch.

- What things do they like or dislike touching?
- Do they have anything which they touch for luck or for comfort? (Touching wood, a comfort blanket, a special toy.)
- Do they have anything which they avoid touching? (Not stepping on cracks, missing a particular stair.)
- Do they know any places which people visit especially to touch things? (Kissing the Blarney stone, pilgrimages to shrines.)
- Are there times when touch has made them feel better?

 ## LISTENING

Introduce and read the following story.

A SPECIAL TOUCH

Maria threw back the blanket. It was dark and everyone else in the house was asleep. She felt ill, her head ached and she was hot. There were pains in her back and legs. It hurt to swallow. She reached out for her bedside light and turned it on. It was only three o'clock in the morning. No wonder it was still dark. Perhaps if she had a drink of water she would feel better, there was a glass in the bathroom. Maria got out of bed and turned on the landing light, but as she did so she suddenly felt that her legs would no longer stay straight. She tried to steady herself on the wall but instead knocked over the table on the landing and fell with a crash to the floor.

In a second her mother was there. She picked Maria up in her arms and half walked

AUTUMN TERM

half carried her to the bedroom. 'My word, you feel as if you're on fire,' Mum said. She sat Maria on a chair with a dressing gown tucked around her. 'Now let's get this bed straight for a start. It looks as if you've been having a fight with the duvet cover.' Mum fetched a clean under sheet and pillow case from the airing cupboard. She stripped and remade the bed and helped Maria into a clean nightie. Then she came back with a cool flannel and wiped Maria's hot head and gently brushed her hair back from her face. 'I'm going to fetch you a drink and a tablet to help reduce this temperature,' said Mum, 'I won't be long. 'Maria rested on the pillows. The sheets felt cool and crisp and her face was no longer sticky.

Mum was soon back. She handed Maria the tablet and a glass of cool iced lemon. The ice was so soothing to Maria's dry throat. Mum sat on the edge of the bed and held Maria's hand. 'Now lie back and see if you can sleep. I'll just sit here for a while'. Maria closed her eyes. It was so comforting to feel Mum's hand. Her head still ached but she knew she was feeling better already.

 ## MUSIC AND REFLECTION

Introduce the music and ask the children to think about how Maria felt at the start of the story and what experiences of touch helped her to feel better.

 ## HYMN

Jesus' hands were kind hands *(Someone's singing Lord No. 33)*

 ## PRAYER

We thank you God for the delight of touching.
The feel of cool crisp sheets.
Of sand beneath our feet.
Of water running through our fingers.
The roughness of bricks or the bark of a tree.
The smoothness of glass or polished metal.
The warmth of a fire on a winter's day and the refreshment of a cool breeze in the heat of summer.
For the kind touch of hands which help us.
For all these gifts we give you thanks.

Amen

 ## CLOSING REFRAIN

Shalom *(Come and Praise No. 141)*

TRAVELLING FURTHER
Continue reflecting on the theme of touching.

In your class or year worship time try to:

- Present opportunities to explore a variety of tactile experiences.
- Encourage an appreciation of the gift of touch.
- Help the children to recognize when touch can heal and when it can harm.

With the children make a collection of things they enjoy touching (Stones, tree bark, feathers, sand, fabric, plastics, metals). Include a variety of textures (Hard, soft, smooth, furry, slippery). Give plenty of opportunity to share and discuss the experience of touch.

Make a book of 'touch games'. Ask the children to describe by picture diagram or words the games they play which involve touch (What's the time Mr Wolf? Cat and mouse, Tag statues, Chain tag, blind tag).

Make a tactile picture (use pasta shapes, seeds, shells, textiles, beads etc. stick to a card base).

Look at some of the healing miracles of Jesus and see how he used touch to reassure and comfort. The healing of the leper (Matthew 8.1 – 4). The woman who touched Jesus and was healed (Mark 5.24 – 34).

Explore how touch can be used to comfort or to restore physical health (hugs for reassurance, the work of physiotherapists and masseurs).

This could be an opportunity to look at the area of abuse and perhaps raise the issue of touching which is not comfortable.

USEFUL RESOURCES

Let's Play Together by Mildred Masheder Green (published by Green Print ISBN 1-85425-009-4).
Kids can say No by Rolph Harris (Video for children concerning child abuse).
Beyond the Scare (Video training programme for teachers).
Both videos may be purchased from 183 Drury Lane, London, WC2B 5QF, Telephone 071 240 8777, or for hire from Concord Films: Telephone 0473 715754. These may also be available from some resource centres.

AUTUMN TERM

ON THE HOME STRAIGHT
Collective worship for the end of the week

GATHERING
Remind the children of the theme of touch.

LISTENING
Invite a physiotherapist from a hospital or sports centre to demonstrate how touch and massage can ease or heal stress and pain. Alternatively a class could present a play about a healing miracle of Jesus, a demonstration of touch games, or a presentation of items which they enjoy touching.

MUSIC AND REFLECTION
Introduce the music and choose a direction for reflection linked to the experience of the Listening section.

HYMN
Hands to work and feet to run *(Someone's Singing Lord No. 21)*

PRAYER
Lord, you used your hands to heal and comfort others. Help us to be aware of how we can touch the lives of others by our kindness.

Amen

CLOSING REFRAIN
Shalom *(Come and Praise No. 141)*

AUTUMN TERM
THEME 3: *Food*

Week 1
Food glorious food.

Week 2
Who helped make the
breakfast?

Week 3
Fair Shares

Some schools may wish to adapt aspects of the work in this theme
for a harvest thanksgiving service.

Checklist for Hymn Practice

The super supper march *(Apuskiddu Songs for Children No. 6)*
Thank you, Lord *(Come and Praise No. 32)*

We thank you Lord *(Come and Praise No. 136)*
Here is the farmer – to the tune of 'Here we go round the mulberry bush'.

When God made the garden of creation *(Come and Praise No. 16)*
The sharing bread *(Come and Praise No. 139)*

THEME 3: Week 1

THEME FOR THE WEEK
Food glorious food

AIM: To help children to appreciate the varieties of taste and texture of food and to realize how sharing a meal can be an important way of expressing a friendship.

SETTING OUT
Collective worship for the beginning of the week

 GATHERING

Ask the children about the food they eat and like or dislike.

- What did they eat for breakfast?
- Have they brought anything for their mid-morning break?
- Do they know what they will be eating at lunch time?
- What is their favourite meal?
- Is there any food which they dislike eating?

 LISTENING

Tell the following story:

MIDNIGHT FEAST

Bill woke up and wriggled in his bed. Something was wrong. Was he too hot? No. Was he too cold? No, that wasn't the problem. He was hungry. Bill clutched his stomach. Yes, he was definitely hungry. He swung his legs over the side of the bunk bed and slid down the ladder. He grabbed his dressing gown and pulled on his slippers. Creeping very quietly past his parents bedroom, he slipped stealthily down the stairs and into the kitchen. Pushkin, the cat, opened a sleepy eye as Bill turned on the light. The cat yawned, stretched and sat up in the cane chair by the door.

'I've come down for a little snack,' explained Bill, walking over to the fridge. Bill opened the fridge door and Pushkin walked leisurely across the kitchen and sat looking into the packed shelves. 'Now what do I really fancy?' said Bill to himself.

'I would recommend a toasted sandwich with ham,' said Pushkin.

▬ Autumn Term ▬

'Sounds good to me,' said Bill, as he switched on the sandwich maker and started to cut the bread. It was only as he was tucking into the second sandwich, and feeding Pushkin with scraps of ham, that Bill pondered on the fact that Pushkin had spoken. 'It's just because it's the middle of the night,' Bill explained to himself. 'I'm imagining things.'

Just then Pushkin said, 'I always think a sandwich is much improved by washing it down with a glass of cold milk. Although, speaking personally, I think glasses are vastly over-rated and would prefer my milk in a saucer — if you wouldn't mind.'

'No trouble at all', Bill heard himself saying, as he poured a large glass of frothy milk for himself and a saucer for Pushkin.

Pushkin washed his whiskers carefully and licked his white fur bib. 'If you should still be feeling peckish,' said Pushkin, 'a refreshing snack is red salmon, mashed with a sprinkling of salt and pepper, served with very thin slices of brown bread and butter. I think you'll find a small tin of salmon at the back of the larder on the top shelf. Please don't bother to cut any bread and butter for me. I shall be quite content with the salmon,' the cat continued, as Bill tousled with the tin opener. Bill followed Pushkin's instructions and sat down to eat the salmon while Pushkin munched appreciatively at his portion in the cat bowl. Having licked the very last flake of salmon from around the bowl, Pushkin arched his back in a contented stretch. 'Now to complete a little night snack, such as this, I think there is nothing so enjoyable as a morsel of tasty cheese,' said Pushkin. 'You'll find the cheese on the second shelf of the fridge. There is Brie or Camembert there, I believe, but I think nothing beats a good English Cheddar. I never touch anything else.' As Bill diced the Cheddar into tiny pieces for Pushkin, he did wonder how the cat had become so knowledgeable about cheeses. In fact, he was beginning to wonder about several things when the door of the kitchen swung open.

'Bill! What on earth are you doing down here in the middle of the night, and what have you been eating? My goodness you'll be sick,' said Bill's mother.

'Well, I haven't eaten it all myself,' said Bill, looking around. But Pushkin, who was just jumping back into the cane chair and curling up for a sleep, just blinked his eyes and said not a word.

 ## MUSIC AND REFLECTION

Introduce the music and ask the children to think about some of the things Bill and Pushkin had eaten during the night and consider what they would choose for a midnight feast.

 ## HYMN

The super supper march *(Apuskiddu. Songs for children No. 6)*

AUTUMN TERM

PRAYER

Thank you God for the gift of food.
Thank you for all the different tastes and textures we enjoy.
The crunchiness of fresh bread. The clean fresh taste of an apple.
The sharp tang of lemon. The sweetness of honey.
Help us this week to become more aware of all the enjoyment we have from your gift of food.

Amen

CLOSING REFRAIN

Shalom *(Come and Praise No. 141)*

TRAVELLING FURTHER
Continue to reflect on the theme of food.

In your class or year worship time try to:
● Develop a sense of enjoyment of food.
● Give opportunities to experience different tastes and textures of food.
● Develop an appreciation of cooking and presenting food well.
● Talk about meal times being an occasion for conversation, fellowship and friendship.
● Think about occasions when meals have a special significance.

Tell the story of the hospitality of Abraham (Genesis 18.1 – 8) or the story of the widow who shared her food with Elijah (1 Kings 17. 8 – 16).

Make a class recipe book of favourite meals. Give instructions for cooking and illustrate the book with drawings.

With the children devise a food quiz. Give the children different foods to taste and ask them to define the taste and texture (Sweet, sour, bitter, smooth, lumpy, hot, cold, spicey, bland).

Prepare a class tea party: encourage the children to make decorated paper plates, decorations for the table and to prepare simple food.

Make a class collage of favourite meals. Each child could prepare their collage on their own paper plate. *(These plates could be used in the Setting Out worship for 'Fair Shares'.)*

Find out about how we taste and digest food.

AUTUMN TERM

ON THE HOME STRAIGHT
Collective worship for the end of the week

 ## GATHERING
Remind the children of the theme of the week.

LISTENING
Arrange for a class or group to present something of their work or demonstrate how to prepare a simple meal. If your school is in a multi-faith area it may be possible to invite a member of the Sikh community to talk about the place of hospitality at the *Gurdwara* (House of God).

 ## HYMN
Thank you, Lord (*Come and Praise No. 32*)

PRAYER
For all the gifts of food we have enjoyed this week:
For the gift of taste in all its variety.
For the pleasure of sharing meals with our family or friends.
For the work of all those who have prepared our food this week.
We give thanks.

Amen

 ## CLOSING REFRAIN
Shalom (*Come and Praise No. 141*)

■■■■■■■ **AUTUMN TERM** ■■■■■■■

THEME 3: Week 2

THEME FOR THE WEEK
Who helped make the breakfast?

AIM: **To help children to understand where food comes from and to appreciate the work of the many people who provide our daily bread.**

SETTING OUT
Collective worship for the beginning of the week (This will need preparation beforehand.)

✖↓✘ GATHERING

Have a table already prepared as for breakfast, set with plates, bowls, mugs, cutlery and suitable food. Have available cereals, milk, sugar, tea, coffee, fruit juice, bread, butter and marmalade. *(These instructions are for a western style meal but it may be more appropriate for your school to choose a different pattern.)*
Draw attention to the breakfast table and all the things ready for breakfast. Ask the children:

- Who helped prepare breakfast in their homes?
- Who laid the table?
- Who made the toast?
- Who made the drinks?
- Who cleared up the dishes?

LISTENING

Invite someone to come to breakfast and as they eat each food lead a discussion about where the food came from. For example; as the milk is poured on the cereal . . . the milk came from the milkman / supermarket / milk lorry / dairy farmer / cow.

As the bread is cut . . . the bread came from the shop assistant / supermarket / delivery lorry / baker / miller / grain merchant / farmer.

MUSIC AND REFLECTION

Introduce the music and invite the children to think about the food they will eat during the day and to give thanks for the people who bring us our food.

46

AUTUMN TERM

HYMN

We thank you Lord (Come and Praise No. 136)

PRAYER

We remember with thanks all those who work to bring us our daily bread.
For farmers in this country and in lands far away.
For all those who transport our food by air, sea, road or rail.
For those who package our food and those who sell it in the shops.
For those who cook our meals and feed us each and every day.

Amen

CLOSING REFRAIN

Shalom (Come and Praise No. 141)

TRAVELLING FURTHER

Use some of the following ideas to continue reflection on the theme of food.

In your class or year worship time try to:

● Develop an awareness of the vast areas of the world from which we glean our food.
● Think about the variety of work which is involved in bringing food to our tables.
● Foster an appreciation for the work of others in providing our daily bread.

Make a collage showing the journey of either bread, milk, sugar or cereal from field to table.

Collect labels from tins and packets and mount them around a map of the world to show their countries of origin.

Find out about tea, coffee or cereal farming.

Prepare a mime with simple costumes and props to illustrate the song below sung to the tune of 'Here we go round the mulberry bush.'

Here is the farmer who grows the seed, grows the seed, grows the seed.
Here is the farmer who grows the seed which gives us the bread for breakfast.
Here is the miller who grinds the corn . . .
Here is the baker who kneads the dough . . .
Here is the driver delivering the bread . . .
Here is the assistant who sells the bread . . .

USEFUL RESOURCES

There are some excellent publications from Oxfam. The following are particularly helpful and are available from Youth and Education Programme, Oxfam, 274 Banbury Road, Oxford OX2 7JF Telephone 0865 311311:
The world in a supermarket bag.
Food for thought.
Go bananas. Sowing and harvesting.

ON THE HOME STRAIGHT
Collective worship for the end of the week

GATHERING

Remind the children that they have been thinking about where their food comes from and the people involved in producing it.

LISTENING

Arrange for someone involved in the production of food to visit and talk about their work. This could be a farmer, lorry driver, baker or shop manager. Alternatively allow some of the children to report on their work.

MUSIC AND REFLECTION

Introduce the music and choose a direction for reflection which is linked to the experience of the Listening section.

HYMN

Use the song 'Here is the Farmer', prepared in 'Travelling Further'.

PRAYER

For all who work to bring us food
to fill our cups and plates full,
For all who toil and shop and cook
Lord make us truly grateful.

Amen

CLOSING REFRAIN

Shalom *(Come and Praise No. 141)*

■ Autumn Term ■

THEME 3: Week 3

THEME FOR THE WEEK
Fair shares

AIM: **To help the children begin to understand the causes of hunger and to affirm the hope of overcoming the problem.**

SETTING OUT
Collective worship for the beginning of the week (This will need preparation beforehand.)

GATHERING

Introduce and talk about the idea of sharing fairly.

- How do they share the equipment in the classroom?
- How do they share toys?
- How would they share six sweets between three people fairly?
- How would they share one apple between two people fairly?
- Explain that you are going to show how the food of the world is shared out. Ask the children to watch and judge if they think it is fair.

LISTENING

This activity is not difficult but a little practice beforehand would be advisable. You will need twelve paper plates. If possible decorate these with a collage or drawing of a meal. Plates could be those prepared as an activity in the 'Food, glorious food section'.

Show children one plate of food and explain that one plate represents enough food for one person to remain fit and healthy. Show the children the pile of twelve plates and tell them that it represents all the food available in the world.

Choose ten children to stand up and explain that they represent all the people in the world.

Ask another child to share out the food of the world fairly. There will be two plates left over. Help the children to understand that there is enough food for everyone and to spare.

Collect in the plates.

■ Autumn Term ■

Ask the children why they think some people are still hungry in the world (drought, flood, no land to grow food, no work to earn money to buy food, too poorly paid to afford food).

Ask the children to guess how many of the ten representing the whole world are well fed like us. Tell them that only three are well fed. Move three slightly apart.

Ask the children how many plates of food we had (12). Ask the children to guess how many of the plates go to the seven poorly fed (3). After they have guessed give them three plates to share between the seven.

Ask how many plates are left for the well fed three (9). Share out the nine plates between the three people.

Ask the children 'How many plates do we need each?' (1) 'What do you think the well fed people do with the food they do not need?' (Eat too much, throw it away, store it?)

Discuss with the children how they think a loving God would like us to distribute the food and then re-distribute the plates.

Discuss what could be done with the two extra plates. (Stored for emergency?)

 ## MUSIC AND REFLECTION

Introduce the music and ask the children to think of ways we can help those who have no food.

 ## HYMN

When God made the garden of creation *(Come and Praise No. 16)*

 ## PRAYER

Lord, help us to understand what it is like to be hungry.
Give us imagination to see the needs of those less fortunate than ourselves.
Grant us strength and determination to work for fair shares of the food of the world.

Amen

 ## CLOSING REFRAIN

Shalom *(Come and Praise No. 141)*

TRAVELLING FURTHER

Use some of the following ideas to reflect on the theme of 'Fair Shares'.

In your year or class worship time try to:

- Develop an understanding of the causes of hunger (war, not enough land to grow food, natural disasters, failure of rain, insufficient seed, lack of equipment, lack of knowledge or irrigation), and the results of hunger (weakness, inability to work, falling prey to diseases).
- Develop a sense of care and responsibility for the world community and for sharing the resources of the world justly.
- Foster a positive attitude to solving the problems of world hunger.
- Encourage an interest in the work of aid agencies which aim to combat the problems of hunger.

Organise a visiting speaker from Oxfam, Christian Aid or Save the Children Fund.

Organise a class, year or school sale to raise money for one of the aid charities.

Make a collage to illustrate the following verse:

> God has given us a planet where there's food a-plenty.
> Let's all share it with each other so that none go empty.

Tell or act out the story of the unjust King and Naboth's vineyard (1 Kings 21.1 – 21).

Tell or act out the story of the boy who shared his lunch (John 6. 1 – 13).

USEFUL ADDRESSES

Oxfam: Oxfam House, 274 Banbury Road, Oxford OX2 7JF.
Christian Aid: Inter Church House, 35-41 Lower Marsh Street,
London SE1 7RL Telephone 071 620 4444.
Save the Children Fund: Mary Datchelor House, 17 Grove Lane, Camberwell, London SE5 8RD Telephone 071 703 5400.

AUTUMN TERM

ON THE HOME STRAIGHT
Collective worship for the end of the week

GATHERING

Remind the children that they have been thinking about what it means to share food fairly. Talk about some of the work and activities the children have done during the week. Introduce the story of the boy who shared his lunch.

LISTENING

Tell in your own words, or read the story, of the feeding of the five thousand (John 6.1 – 13). Alternatively a class or group may like to act this out. Rolls and 'fish' can be made from a simple scone recipe.

MUSIC AND REFLECTION

Introduce the music and ask children to reflect on the story. How did the miracle happen? Does God need our co-operation for miracles to happen? Would it be a miracle if the world shared its food more fairly?

HYMN

The sharing bread *(Come and Praise No. 139)*

PRAYER

Lord Jesus, you showed your concern for the hunger of those around you. Make us aware of the needs of all the children in the world. Help us to be generous, so that the food of the earth may be shared fairly between all people, and all may know of your love and care.

Amen

CLOSING REFRAIN

Shalom *(Come and Praise No. 141)*

AUTUMN TERM
THEME 4: *Lights*

Week 1
Varieties of Lights.

Week 2
Lights of the World.

Week 3
Celebrations of Light.

Checklist for Hymn Practice

I watch the sunrise *(Alleluya, 77 songs for thinking people No. 15)*
When night arrives *(Come and Praise No. 92)*

This little light of mine *(Alleluya, 77 songs for thinking people No. 14)*
Jesus bids us shine *(Junior Praise No. 128)*

Now light one thousand Christmas lights *(Carol, Gaily Carol No. 39)*
Flickering candles in the night *(Come and Praise No. 114)*

■■ AUTUMN TERM ■■

THEME 4: Week 1

THEME FOR THE WEEK
Varieties of lights

AIM: To help the children become more aware of the varieties of light and begin to be aware of its symbolic significance.

SETTING OUT
Collective worship for the beginning of the week

 ## GATHERING

Read the following:

In the beginning of Creation, when God made heaven and earth, the earth was without form and void, with darkness over the form of the abyss, and a mighty wind that swept over the surface of the waters. God said 'Let there be light', and there was light; and God saw that the light was good, and he separated light from darkness. He called the light day and the darkness night.

(Genesis 1.1 – 5)

Explain that the theme for the next three weeks is 'Light'.

LISTENING

Read the following poem and ask the children to identify as many kinds of light as possible.

SUNBRIGHT DAYLIGHT

Sunbright daylight,
Stars in the darkest night,
Glow-worm, candle light,
Christmas tree and birthday lights:

Shop lights glare white,
Posters neon-bright,
Headlight, traffic lights,
Ambulance with flashing light:

■ AUTUMN TERM ■

Ship lights, flare white,
Lighthouse, guiding bright,
Train lights, station lights,
Signal box and warning lights:

Sparklers, match light,
Rockets – what a sight!
Look out – jumping light,
Golden rain on bonfire night:

Floodlight, spotlight,
Usherette's torch light,
Swing-boat, hold on tight,
Roundabout and fairground lights:

Moonlight, space flight,
Beacon, satellite,
Red light, from a height –
Aeroplane and runway lights:

Coach light, lamp light,
Porch light, home in sight,
Bath light, bedside light
Put it out and say good night!

Cecily Taylor From *New Horizons*

MUSIC AND REFLECTION

Introduce the music and ask the children to reflect on all the variety of lights which they will experience during the day and night.

HYMN

I watch the sunrise (*Alleluya, 77 songs for thinking people No. 15*)

PRAYER

God, the creator of both darkness and light,
We praise you for all the wonders of light around us.
For the soft lights of dawn and twilight, for candle light and moonlight.
For the sparkle of the sunlight on the sea and the stars in the night sky.
For the welcoming lights of our homes on dark evenings.
For the comfort of nightlights by our bedside.
For bright lights which tell of celebration and fun.
For lights which guide us in the darkness and warn us of any dangers.
Lord, for the light of the world, we give you thanks.

Amen

CLOSING REFRAIN

Shalom *(Come and Praise No. 141)*

TRAVELLING FURTHER

Continue reflection on the theme of light

In your worship time try to:

- Help the children become aware of the wide varieties of lights and their purposes.
- Foster an awareness of how lights can guide, warn, comfort or be a source of celebration.
- Encourage thought about light as a symbol.

Make an exhibition entitled 'Varieties of Lights.' With the class collect as many types of light as possible: torches, flashlights, candles, nightlights, oil lamps, Davy lamps etc.

Help the children to appreciate the different purposes of each light: lights which guide, lights which warn, lights which comfort, lights which celebrate.

Make a frieze showing as many types of lights as possible.

Find out about the history of lighting. Different groups could find out about lighting by oil, gas or electricity.

Use a lighted candle as a focus for a short period. Ask the group to share their observations of the light and their thoughts.

Devise a short shadow puppet play: cut silhouette shapes from black card, attach to sticks or wires and operate against a screen illuminated from behind.

Discuss, in groups, the contrast between a walk taken in the light and the same walk taken in the dark.

AUTUMN TERM

ON THE HOME STRAIGHT
Collective worship for the end of the week

GATHERING
Remind the children of the theme of 'Light'.

LISTENING
Arrange for a class, or group, to present some of their work or read the following poem about varieties of Light.

VARIETIES OF LIGHT

The lighthouse gleams across the silvery waters.
The searchlight scans the darkness of the sky.
The red lights of the traffic lights are warning us to stop.
We give our thanks for lights protecting us.

The torchlight beams along the path before us.
The car lights pierce the shadows of the road.
The lights from nearby windows beckon welcoming us home.
We give our thanks for lights which guide our way.

The fireworks sparkle brilliantly and clearly.
The candles flicker on the birthday cake.
The lights along the seashore glitter cheerfully and bright.
We give our thanks for lights which celebrate.

The sun has gone and shadows fall around us.
The silvery moon and stars light up the sky.
The earth waits patiently to greet the sunrise in the east.
We give our thanks to him who gave us light.

MUSIC AND REFLECTION
Introduce the music and ask the children to reflect on all they have discovered about light during the week.

AUTUMN TERM

HYMN

When night arrives *(Come and Praise No. 92)*

PRAYER

For all lights which guide us,
For all lights which comfort us,
For all lights which protect us from danger,
For all lights which bring us joy and celebration,
For the light of the world,
We thank you God.

Amen

CLOSING REFRAIN

Shalom *(Come and Praise No. 141)*

================ **AUTUMN TERM** ================

THEME 4: Week 2

THEME FOR THE WEEK
Lights of the world

AIM: **To help children understand the symbol of Christ as a light and to see how people can be seen as lights of the world.**

SETTING OUT
Collective worship for the beginning of the week

 ## GATHERING

Read the following:
Jesus said: 'I am the light of the world. No follower of mine shall wander in the dark; he shall have the light of life'.

(John 8.12)

You are light for all the world. A town that stands on a hill cannot be hidden. When a lamp is lit it is not put under the meal-tub, but on the lamp stand, where it gives light to everyone in the house. And you, like the lamp, must shed light among your fellows, so that, when they see the good you do, they may give praise to your Father in heaven.

(Matthew 5.14 – 16)

Explore briefly how Christ was a light in the world, guiding, warning, comforting, sharing joys and sorrows. Explain that the story is about someone who also tried to bring comfort and hope to the world.

LISTENING

THE WHITE FLAME

Over one hundred years ago, there was a family living in Shropshire called Jebb. Mr and Mrs Jebb were very happy when they had a baby girl. They decided to call her a very unusual name: they called her Eglantyne. As they looked into her cradle and admired their beautiful daughter, Mr and Mrs Jebb could never have guessed that she would grow up to help millions of babies and children throughout the world.

Eglantyne was a very lucky baby. She had been born into a wealthy family and always

AUTUMN TERM

had lovely clothes, plenty to eat, a warm home and probably a governess to teach her. If she was ill, her mother would send for a doctor to help her get better.

It was not the same for all the children in England at that time. Poor children were often ragged, cold, without enough clothes and frequently hungry. Some of them had to beg and work for long hours in order to survive. When they were ill they could not afford to go to the doctor for help and medicine because there was no health service in those days.

As Eglantyne grew up she had many advantages. She was clever and went to Oxford University to study history. When she had finished her degree she told her parents that she wanted to teach. 'Teach!' exclaimed Mr Jebb. 'What a strange thing to choose to do'. Teaching was not considered 'ladylike' work at that time and Eglantyne's family and friends were amazed. Despite all their opposition Eglantyne began to teach. Many of the children who were in her class were very poor. Eglantyne noticed how thin their clothes were even in the depths of winter. She realised that they were often hungry and because of that they were frequently ill and could rarely concentrate on their lessons. Moreover their parents often wanted them to leave school as they needed their children to work to help buy food.

After a year of teaching Eglantyne became ill herself. She had to give up her work but was still concerned for the children, not only those she knew about in England but also those she heard about in other parts of the world. In 1912, a war broke out in the Balkans. Eglantyne heard how the children were suffering as a result of losing their homes and families. As soon as the war had finished she travelled to the war torn areas taking food and clothing to refugees and war victims. She saw at first hand how children suffer so dreadfully in war. She saw many children who were hungry, injured or ill and wrote, 'Every war, just or unjust, is a war against the child'.

When in 1914 the First World War broke out Eglantyne was very worried for she knew that all children in the countries involved in the war would suffer and that thousands of them would be desperately in need of help. Determined to help the children as soon as the war was over, she said to her sister Dorothy, 'We can't just do nothing'.

'But Eglantyne – what can we do so far away and with relatively so little money,' said Dorothy.

'We can set up a fund and ask people to give money to help buy food, clothing and medicine. If only they knew what it was like I'm sure they would want to help. We shall call it the 'Save The Children Fund'. So, with Dorothy's help Eglantyne set about organising a big meeting in London. She hired the Albert Hall and invited many, many people and on the 19th of May she made her first appeal for the The Fund.

Much to Eglantyne's delight money was soon pouring in. The Miner's Federation contributed ten thousand pounds but Eglantyne was just as excited and pleased with tiny donations. 'Look at this,' she cried, showing a crumpled envelope to her sister. In the envelope was 2s 6d (12p) with a letter from a little girl explaining that she had sent it, 'so that you can feed all the starving children'. During the next two years almost one million pounds was raised.

From then on Eglantyne worked tirelessly to raise money to help children all over the world. Food, clothing, medicine and supplies were sent to refugees in Armenia, to victims of earthquakes in Tokyo and to starving children in Russia. Always Eglantyne championed the rights of children, of whatever race, nationality or creed to a healthy life, education and care.

AUTUMN TERM

Eglantyne was never very fit herself. All her life she suffered from a thyroid disease but she never allowed her frailty to deter her work. Her friends called her, 'The White Flame,' because she was so pale, but always spreading the light and warmth of loving concern. When she died, at the age of fifty-two, Eglantyne had begun an organisation which today has over 800 branches throughout the world: the 'White Flame' had lit beacons of hope for children everywhere.

MUSIC AND REFLECTION

Introduce the music and ask the children to reflect on how the life and work of Eglantyne had spread the light of comfort, joy, hope and had guided those around her.

HYMN

This little light of mine *(Alleluya, 77 songs for thinking people No. 14)*

PRAYER

Thank you God for all those people who shine as lights in the dark world. For those who bring hope to the lonely, comfort to the sad and joy to the despairing.
Make us lights which shine with the warmth of your love.

Amen

CLOSING REFRAIN

Shalom *Come and Praise No. 141)*

TRAVELLING FURTHER

In your worship time try to:

- Develop an awareness of how the action of people can bring light.
- Awaken a sense of light as a symbol of enlightenment.
- Encourage the children to think of ways in which they can 'shine as lights in the world'.

Find out about some 'lights of the world' (e.g. Elizabeth Fry, William Wilberforce, Mother Theresa of Calcutta).

Tell the story of Florence Nightingale, 'The Lady with the Lamp'.

■ AUTUMN TERM ■

Tell the story of Christ's presentation in the Temple: a light to lighten the Gentiles (Luke 2. 21 – 35).

Draw a very large candle and divide it into bands with one band for each child. Ask each child to decorate their band with a story or picture of how they can bring light (comfort, hope joy, enlightenment) to others. Stick the completed bands on the class candle under the heading 'Shine as a light in the world.'

Obtain a reproduction of the picture by W. Holman Hunt 'The Light of the World' *(obtainable from NCEC)*. Around the picture ask the children to write or draw occasions when Christ brought light to those around Him.

USEFUL BOOKS

Florence Nightingale by Nina Morgan, Life series (published by Wayland). *In His Service* Books 1, 2 and 3 (published by Religious and Moral Education Press).
'Faith in Action series' (published by Religious and Moral Education Press). (Stories of people who have worked among the poor and the sick.)

ON THE HOME STRAIGHT
Collective worship for the end of the week

GATHERING

Light a candle and say:
'Jesus said, "I am the light of the world. Let your light so shine that people may see your good works and glorify your Father who is in Heaven" '.

LISTENING

Select some readings from the Bible:

The people who walked in darkness have seen a great light.
They lived in a land of shadows but now light is shining on them. *(Isaiah 9.2)*

The Lord said to me . . .
I will always make you a light to the nations – so that all the world may be saved.
(part of Isaiah 49.6)

The Lord is my light and salvation; I will fear no one. *(Psalm 27.1)*

Autumn Term

But if we live in the light – just as he is in the light – then we have a fellowship with one another.

(part of 1 John 1.7)

Whoever loves his brother lives in the light, and so there is nothing in him that will cause someone else to sin.

(1 John 2.10)

MUSIC AND REFLECTION

Introduce the music and ask the children to think about how they could be lights in the world.

HYMN

Jesus bids us shine *(Junior Praise No. 128)*

PRAYER

Thou whose almighty word
Chaos and darkness heard
And took their flight;
Hear us we humbly pray
And where the Gospel day
Sheds not its glorious ray,
Let there be light.

Amen

CLOSING REFRAIN

Shalom *(Come and Praise No. 141)*

THEME 4: Week 3

THEME FOR THE WEEK
Celebrations of light

AIM: To explore how the gift of light has been a part of celebrations for many ages and how light has a symbolic place in many world religions.

SETTING OUT
Collective worship for the beginning of the week (This will need preparation beforehand)

 GATHERING

Have ready a selection of 'celebratory' lights: cake candles, an Advent candle, candles in a table decoration, Christmas tree lights.

Show the lights to the children and talk about the use of lights in celebrations. Introduce the story about a celebration of light which happens each year in Sweden.

 LISTENING

ST LUCY'S DAY

'Wake up Ingrid!' said Gustav. 'Wake up or we will be too late.' Ingrid pulled the duvet further over her head.

'Go away little brother. Why are you disturbing me at this hour of the morning. It is still dark.'

'Have you forgotten what day it is?' said Gustav. 'It's the 13th of December, St Lucy's day and you are to be St Lucy. Hurry or Mother and Father will stir before we have time to surprise them'.

Ingrid sat up in bed and shook her blonde hair. She reached out for her hairbrush and ribbon and tied her plaits in place.

'Here, let me help you,' said Gustav, handing Ingrid the long white dress. Ingrid slipped the robe on and tied the red sash around her waist. 'Where is my head-dress?' she asked.

'I have left it in the kitchen with the tray. It is all ready and the kettle is on to make the coffee,' said Gustav.

■ AUTUMN TERM ■

Ingrid and Gustav crept out of their bedroom and downstairs into the kitchen. Whilst Gustav made a pot of coffee and put some special buns on the tray, Ingrid arranged her head-dress. It was a wreath of greenery in which she had placed five tall white candles. They were electric candles as Ingrid did not want to use ordinary candles in case they caught fire.

'Ready? Now careful as you take the tray,' warned Gustav, 'I will go ahead and open the door as we sing the song we made up'. The two children walked up the stairs and into their parents bedroom singing: 'Here comes St Lucy, wake from the dark. We bring you light and food for your heart.'

'Welcome little St Lucy,' shouted Mother, as father took the tray from Ingrid's hands. The children clambered into bed beside their parents and they all enjoyed the coffee and saffron buns.

'Dad, why do we celebrate St Lucy's day?' asked Gustav.

'Oh, it's a very old tradition in Sweden', said Father. Legends say that St Lucy used to take food to the first Christians when they were hiding in the catacombs in Rome.'

'She wore the candles on her head, so that her hands were free to carry the food,' explained Mother, 'but there have always been celebrations of light at this time of the year long before even St Lucy'.

'I suppose people were always glad to think that the long dark days of winter would be coming to an end and the warmth of the sun would soon return,' said Father. 'St Lucy is a reminder of all the hope which light brings and, when we reach this time of the year, we can also begin to think of the coming of Jesus – who came as a light to the world'.

 ## MUSIC AND REFLECTION

Introduce the music and ask the children to think of times when they use lights to help them celebrate and especially to think of the ways in which lights are used to celebrate Christmas.

 ## HYMN

Now light one thousand Christmas lights *(Carol, Gaily Carol No. 39)*
Flickering candles in the night *(Come and Praise No. 114)*

 ## PRAYER

We thank you God, for the coming of Jesus at Christmas:
'He came to bring us love and light,
To bring us peace on earth,
So let your candles shine tonight,
And sing with joy and mirth.'

 ## CLOSING REFRAIN

Shalom *(Come and Praise No. 141)*

THEME 4: Week 3

■ Autumn Term ■

TRAVELLING FURTHER

In your worship time try to:

- Explore the religious significance of light
- Explore the celebrations of the winter solstice
- Explore how light is an important symbol in many world religions.

Make an Advent wreath to mark the season of the coming of Christ.

Make Christmas decorations associated with light (decorative candles, paper lanterns, stars).

Find out about festivals of the winter solstice such as the Roman festival of Saturnalia, or the northern European festival of Yule.

Find out about the Jewish festival of Hanukkah or the Hindu festival of *Divali*.

Plan a Christingle service. Details of how to organise this can be obtained from: Christingles, The Children's Society, Edward Rudolf House, Margery St. London WC1X 0JL Telephone 071 837 4299

USEFUL BOOKS AND VIDEOS

Winter Festivals, Seasonal Festivals series (published by Wayland).
Divali, Living Festivals series (published by Religious and Moral Education Press).
Chanukah by Lynne Scholefield (published by the Religious and Moral Education Press).
Video 1, *Living Festivals* includes Chanukah.
Video 2, *Living Festivals* includes Divali, available from Christian Education Movement Videos, Chansitor publications, St Mary's Works, St Mary's Plain, Norwich, NR3 3BH.

AUTUMN TERM

ON THE HOME STRAIGHT
Collective worship for the end of the week

 GATHERING

Read the following Bible extracts:

I, the Lord, will be your eternal light;
The light of my glory will shine on you.   *(Isaiah 60.19)*

I, the Lord, will be your eternal light;
More lasting than the sun and moon.   *(Isaiah 60.20)*

Let us walk in the light which the Lord gives us!   *(Isaiah 2.5)*

 LISTENING

This could be a Christingle service or a presentation of work about one of the festivals of light.
Alternatively the St Lucy legend could be acted out.

 MUSIC AND REFLECTION

Introduce the music and ask the children to reflect on all they have found out about light and celebration this week.

 HYMN

Christmas Time *(Come and Praise No. 127)*

 PRAYER

Lord you came into the world to bring light and peace
Help us to be messengers of light.
May we bring
Warmth to a cold world
Light to a dark world and
Joy to a sad world.

Amen

 CLOSING REFRAIN

Shalom *(Come and Praise No. 141)*

AUTUMN TERM
THEME 5: *Presents*

Week 1
Giving and receiving.

Week 2
Surprises.

Week 3
What can I give him?

Checklist for Hymn Practice

The best gift *(Come and Praise No. 59)*
God is love *(Come and Praise No. 36)*

Joseph is sad as he travels the way *(Carol, Gaily carol No. 5)*
Oh, who would be a shepherd boy *(Carol, Gaily carol No. 32)*

What shall I give to the child in the manger? *(Carol, Gaily carol No. 26)*
The wise may bring their learning *(Come and Praise No. 64)*

■■■■■■■■■ **AUTUMN TERM** ■■■■■■■■■

THEME 5: Week 1

THEME FOR THE WEEK
Giving and receiving

AIM: **To explore the motives behind our giving and what true giving entails.**

SETTING OUT
Collective worship for the beginning of the week

 GATHERING

Discuss with the children what they are hoping to give and receive at Christmas and introduce the theme of 'Presents'.

 LISTENING

THE PERFECT GIFT

Kevin's aunt sat down in the armchair with a big sigh. 'It was such a crush on the train. I thought I would never get here,' she said, 'but I've never missed your birthday yet and here I am. Now, if you could just pass me that bag over there Kevin, the one leaning against my case, I can get out your present.' Kevin carried the bag to his aunt and waited by her side. Dear Aunt Fiona, he thought, she always remembered the family birthdays and always managed to visit them and make the day seem really special.

'Ah! found it at last,' said Aunt Fiona, as she pulled out a large soft parcel from her bag and handed it to Kevin. 'Happy Birthday Kevin. I do hope you like it. I made it myself.' Kevin hugged the parcel to him. There were no hard corners or shapes to give him a clue as to what it might be. He tore off the wrapping paper in a rush and then took a sharp intake of breath. There, before him, was the most amazing jumper Kevin had ever seen.

'Well yes, thank you. It's . . .'

'It's, very unusual – colourful isn't it Kevin?' said his mother, as she came into the room. Kevin could tell from her voice that he was meant to say something appreciative. He looked at the jumper in disbelief. Was he really expected to wear it? It was striped with every conceivable colour: reds and blues alongside purples and yellows, greens and blacks. It was like Joseph's coat of many colours. What would his mates think of him if he went out wearing this?

'Thank you, thank you very much,' he stammered.

'Do try it on. I'm longing to know if it fits,' said his aunt. Kevin had an idea. 'I'll nip upstairs and change right away,' he said. Upstairs he could pull the jumper on, briefly, and then perhaps pretend it was too small or that the arms were too long. But as he walked across the landing, he heard his aunt's voice as she talked with his mother.

'I'm sorry the jumper is such a riot of colour,' she was saying. 'To be honest it was a real problem to afford a present this year, what with my losing my job and money being short. Then I had this idea of making him something out of the small pieces of wool I had in my knitting bag. I must admit it took me ages sorting out all the pieces and then joining in each new length.'

Upstairs, Kevin looked again at the jumper and suddenly saw it in a different way. He thought of all the care his aunt must have taken to make it. The hours she must have spent and her hopes that he would like it. It was no longer a hideously garish jumper but a gift of love which, there was no way, he could or would refuse. He pulled the jumper over his head. It was a bit big and the arms were too long, as his aunt remarked when he went to show her, but Kevin insisted that it was fine. Even when his friend, Jim, came to collect him for football practice, Kevin kept the jumper on. 'It's a really smashing present,' said Kevin, giving Aunt Fiona a hug.

'You really do like it then?' said Aunt Fiona. 'That's made my day,' and she leant contentedly, in the armchair, sipping her cup of tea.

MUSIC AND REFLECTION

Introduce the music and ask the children to think about how the jumper was a gift of care and love. Did Kevin give his aunt a present too?

HYMN

The best gift *(Come and Praise No. 59)*

PRAYER

Teach us good Lord, to give with love and thoughtfulness.
Teach us good Lord, to choose the ways we give carefully.
Teach us to give with a generous heart and to receive with joyfulness.

Amen

CLOSING REFRAIN

Shalom *(Come and Praise No. 141)*

THEME 5: Week 1

AUTUMN TERM

TRAVELLING FURTHER
In your worship time try to:

- Examine Christ's attitude to giving.
- Explore what true giving entails.
- Examine the place of receiving gifts.
- Look at the type of giving which entails the giving of time, effort and love rather than objects.

Read or tell the story of the widow's mite (Luke 21. 1 – 4) and the story of the woman with the jar of precious ointment (Mark 14. 3 – 9). Discuss what we learn about giving from these stories.

Ask the children to write a story or devise a drama entitled 'The perfect gift.'

Discuss what would be a suitable, but inexpensive, gift for: a newborn baby, a housebound grandfather, a sporting sister, an artistic brother.

Encourage the children to make a simple gift or special Christmas cards for someone in their family.

ON THE HOME STRAIGHT
Collective worship for the end of the week

GATHERING
Continuing the theme of giving and receiving, the following story tells of two people giving to Jesus. In hot and dusty countries it was the custom to wash guests feet as they arrived.

LISTENING
Simon was ambitious. He wanted people to think he was important. He had heard a lot about Jesus of Nazareth and how some people claimed he would be a future leader; so Simon had invited Jesus to a meal alongside some of Simon's influential friends to judge for himself whether this Jesus was a person it would be useful to know.

■ AUTUMN TERM ■

Simon looked with smug satisfaction at the distinguished guests around the table but then, to his horror, a scruffy woman in ragged clothes crept in and knelt at Jesus' feet. Simon recognized her at once. She was very poor and had a terrible reputation in the city. He hoped his guest wouldn't think he had invited her.

Before Simon could do anything, the woman started weeping and as her tears fell over Jesus' feet, she wiped his feet dry with her long hair. Then she pulled out an expensive jar of soothing foot lotion. Simon gasped has she opened the jar and began to pour it onto Jesus' feet and to massage it gently in. 'What extravagance,' thought Simon. 'If Jesus was a person of any prestige he would understand what sort of a woman she is, refuse her gift and save me embarrassment.'

Jesus turned to Simon as if he had heard his thoughts. 'Simon,' he said, 'when I came to your house you did not offer to wash my hot and dusty feet. Indeed you hardly greeted me. But this woman has not stopped washing my feet with her tears. In the past she may have done wrong but can you not see her sorrow? I am glad to accept a gift given with such love and generosity.'

MUSIC AND REFLECTION

Introduce the music and ask the children to reflect on Simon's hospitality and the woman's gift. What did Jesus notice about their giving?

HYMN

God is love *(Come and Praise No. 36)*

PRAYER

Lord Jesus, you came to earth at Christmas time to show us how to love and how to give.

Help us to give love to all we meet and so to show the true meaning of giving.

Amen

CLOSING REFRAIN

Shalom *(Come and Praise No. 141)*

■ AUTUMN TERM ■ ·

THEME 5: Week 2

THEME FOR THE WEEK
Surprises

AIM: **To explore what a surprise means and how we react to surprises.**

SETTING OUT
Collective worship for the beginning of the week

 GATHERING

Remind the children that the current theme is presents and introduce the idea that this week they will be thinking about surprises.

 LISTENING

THE INNKEEPER'S SURPRISE

Simon banged the table with his fist until there was quiet in the inn at Bethlehem. 'Now I just want to say a few words of thanks to all my family and friends who arranged this surprise party for me. I really had no idea it was going to happen.'

'Running an inn you must be used to surprises,' joked Samuel.

'I bet you could tell a tale or two about the surprises you have coped with over the years. Come on Simon, tell us a story about the greatest surprise you have had'.

'Yes, come on,' urged the rest of the party. 'What was the biggest surprise of your life as an innkeeper?'

'Well, now you're really asking,' said Simon. 'Let me think a minute'.

'I bet I know what it was,' ventured Simon's wife Joanna. 'Do you remember years ago when the governor made everyone go back to the town where they had been born to register? Bethlehem was a mad house. People had travelled from all over the countryside around and every inn in the town was full to overflowing.'

'Ah yes wife, that was a surprise, and one I shall never forget.'

'Go on,' the party encouraged. 'Tell us about it'.

Simon looked thoughtful. 'It was evening, dusk had already fallen and a chill wind was beginning to get up. Joanna and I were exhausted. There were so many visitors in Bethlehem. Every room at our inn was full even our own bedroom. The children and Joanna were going to sleep at her parents home across the road there. Then, there was this knocking on the back door, quiet like, but persistent. I was a bit irritable, I can tell you. We had been so busy and Joanna called out to me from the kitchen, "Don't let anyone else in. We have absolutely no room at all." So I went to the door and opened it just a crack and yelled out "No room at our inn. We are full." I was about to slam the door but the sight which met my eyes made me stop in my tracks. There, in the yard, was a slip of a girl slumped across a little donkey. Standing beside her was a man who was holding her tenderly, so that she didn't fall, and whispering gently, "Don't despair Mary. I'm sure we will find shelter tonight, remember the words of the angel: 'Do not be afraid' ". '

'Yes that was her name, Mary, and the man's name was Joseph. Funny we should both remember after all these years,' interrupted Joanna. 'Well I took one look at the lass,' continued Joanna, 'and it was clear to any mother that her baby was about to be born. This was no time to decide if we had room, we had to move fast. But where could we put them?'

'What on earth could you do?' said Samuel.

'Well, before I could think, Joseph started to lead the donkey down to that old shed in the yard, the one we used to keep the animals in. In a matter of minutes he had made a bed for his wife on the straw and tethered his donkey by the door. I took a lantern down and Joanna took them some hot water and a blanket or two and a bit of bread. And that's where their baby was born, in a stable, with the animals manger for his cradle.'

'Well I don't suppose it was the first baby to be born in an unusual place and I don't expect it will be the last,' murmured Samuel.

'Perhaps not,' said Simon, 'but,' he hesitated, 'I can't think that there can be any truth in it, but young Sarah was our maid at the time. You know – helped Joanna around the inn cooked and cleaned a bit. Well, she said that some shepherds from the hills around Bethlehem told her that they had had a vision of angels that very night. Telling them about the baby born in the stable and that some of them even left their sheep and came to see.'

'Well, we all know what shepherds are like,' laughed one of the visitors. 'Did you really believe the tale?'

'But, that wasn't all,' went on Joanna. 'Later, some rich travellers arrived at our door and wanted to see the baby'.

The crowd at the inn laughed, 'Come on Joanna, you're pulling our legs'.

'No,' said Simon, suddenly serious. 'They said they had followed a star which led them to Bethlehem. They believed the baby was very special. Until tonight we have never told anybody about the experience. It was all so mysterious, and certainly a surprise I will always remember. I can't help wanting to know who that baby really was and what happened to him.'

 MUSIC AND REFLECTION

Introduce the music and ask the children to think of the best surprise of their life and to give thanks for it.

AUTUMN TERM

HYMN

Joseph is sad as he travels the way *(Carol, Gaily Carol No. 5)*

PRAYER

Thank you God for the excitement of surprises.
Help us to appreciate the surprises we enjoy.
Help us to see the opportunities in the surprises we do not expect.

Amen

CLOSING REFRAIN

Shalom *(Come and Praise No. 141)*

TRAVELLING FURTHER

In your worship time try to:

- Share the feelings experienced when confronted with a surprise.
- Discuss how surprises can be good or bad.
- Discuss ways of adapting to a variety of surprises
- Explore stories from the Bible where God acted in a surprising way.
- Tell or act out the following stories:

A surprise for Zechariah (Luke 1. 5 – 25).
A surprise for Mary (Luke 1. 26 – 38).
A surprise for the Shepherds (Luke 2. 8 – 20).
A surprise for Joseph (Matthew 2. 13 – 15 and 19 – 23).
A surprise for Simeon and Anna (Luke 2. 25 – 38).

Using three of the stories above make a tryptich entitled 'God of Surprises'.

Write a story or poem entitled 'The greatest surprise I ever had'.

Consider the Nativity narratives in Matthew 1. 18 – 2.23 and Luke 1. 5 – 2.40. In what ways were the events a shock for the people in the stories? Set up an interview with one of the characters and ask a group to interview that character to discover how it felt to be involved in the situation.

ON THE HOME STRAIGHT
Collective worship for the end of the week

 ## GATHERING

Talk about and share some of the children's work on surprises.

 ## LISTENING

Read the story of the angels appearing to the shepherds (Luke 2. 8 – 20).

 ## MUSIC AND REFLECTION

Introduce the music and ask the children to imagine the story they have just heard and to think about the experiences of the shepherds.

 ## HYMN

Oh, who would be a shepherd boy *(Carol, Gaily Carol No. 32)*

 ## PRAYER

God of surprises give us an open heart to welcome all the unexpected things which come to us.
May we be as trusting as Mary,
As courageous as Joseph,
As adventurous as the shepherds who, leaving their sheep on the hillside, followed the message of the angels and found the Christ child in the manger.

Amen

 ## CLOSING REFRAIN

Shalom *(Come and Praise No. 141)*

━━━━━━━ AUTUMN TERM ━━━━━━━

THEME 5: Week 3

THEME FOR THE WEEK
What can I give him?

AIM: **To explore the gifts we can offer to Christ.**

SETTING OUT
Collective worship for the beginning of the week

GATHERING

Remind the children of the story of the shepherds which they heard at the end of last week. Explain that the story they are about to hear is an imaginary one, of what might have happened, but is not a story from the Bible.

LISTENING

THE SMALLEST SHEPHERD'S GIFT

'Now steady, give your grandfather a helping hand over these rocks,' said Joel to Benjamin, as the shepherds hurried down the hillside towards Bethlehem.

'Don't you worry about me Joel,' said Grandfather. 'I've got my crook to support me over the rough patches. Nothing is going to stop me from seeing this baby. Not after all we heard from the angels. What was it they said little Benjamin? Tell me again'.

'They said we would find the Saviour, the Messiah, wrapped in swaddling clothes and lying in a manger,' said Benjamin, as he scurried along.

'Can it really be true? Will we really see the long awaited Saviour, the one so many have longed for?' said David, Benjamin's older brother. 'To think that we are going to see such a special baby! I long to give him a present something he could keep for always.'

'That's a grand idea son,' said Joel, 'and I know what I shall give him. I shall give him this fleece I carry over my shoulder. It is soft and thick and will keep out the cold winter winds from his cradle.'

Little Benjamin listened to his father and wondered what he could give the baby.

'Well,' said David, 'I shall give him this fine ram's horn which I carry at my side. When this is blown, you can hear the sweet sounds right across the valley. As he grows up he can call to his friends with my horn.'

Little Benjamin listened to his brother and wondered what he could give the baby.

■ Autumn Term ■

'Perhaps,' said grandfather, pausing to rest and catch his breath, 'when he grows up, he will need a staff to rest upon, like I am resting now. I will give him this shepherd's crook of mine and he can remember the Psalm "Thy staff and thy crook are my comfort" '. Little Benjamin looked at his grandfather's beautiful crook and he wondered what he could give to the baby.

Suddenly they were there at the door of the stable and the shepherds, so quietly, crept in and knelt down around the manger where the Christ child lay. Without a word Joel tucked his warm fleece around the baby. David placed his horn at the foot of the manger and Grandfather lay his staff on the stable floor by Mary's feet. Little Benjamin stood still, by the stable door, and wondered what he could give to the baby. Just at that moment, the baby stirred and began to cry. Benjamin, without thinking what he was doing, walked over to the manger and began to sing a lullaby in his soft clear voice. He did not remember where the words or music came from but, as he sang, he thought his heart would burst with love for the tiny helpless, crying baby. As Benjamin's voice soared and fell, he suddenly realised that the baby had stopped crying and was looking straight at him. Then Benjamin knew, without any trace of doubt, that he had given the baby the gift he wanted most of all.

MUSIC AND REFLECTION

Introduce the music and ask the children to reflect on the gifts which the shepherds had given to the baby. Ask them to think about what they would like to bring to the manger as their gift?

HYMN

What shall I give to the child in the manger? *(Carol, Gaily Carol No. 26)*

PRAYER

What shall we give to the child in the manger?
Lord Jesus, as we remember your coming at Christmas time as a gift to the world, help us to think of the gifts we can offer you.

Amen

CLOSING REFRAIN

Shalom *(Come and Praise No. 141)*

■ Autumn Term ■

TRAVELLING FURTHER
In your worship time try to:

- Reflect on the gifts we can offer which are not material e.g. gifts of talents, aptitudes and care.
- Help each child to recognise their giftedness and to see it as worth offering.
- Help children to begin to understand that a material gift is only a representation of the real gift of one's love and friendship.
- Help the children to understand giving as a way of expressing love, not power or manipulation.
- Reflect on some stories of giving and what we can learn from the giver:

Tell the story of *Babouska* by Arthur Scholey, and reflect on her attitude to giving. Lion picture story book (published by Lion).

Show the video *The Clown of God* by Tomie de Paola (Weston Wood Studios Ltd. 14 Friday Street, Henley on Thames, Oxfordshire Customer Services Telephone 0491 577033). Reflect on what the clown offers to the Christ child.

Read or tell the story of the Magi (Matthew 2. 1 – 23) and discuss the significance of their presents.

Reflect on the story *The Smallest Shepherd's Gift* and devise a gift the class or group could offer. (This could be a song, a dance, a picture, a model, or something else which affirms their giftedness.)

ON THE HOME STRAIGHT
Collective worship for the end of the week

GATHERING
Share with the children some thoughts on their activities during the weeks worship.

LISTENING
Read, or tell in your own words, the story of the Magi (Matthew 2. 1 – 12). You may like to include some of the 'gifts' the children have prepared.

⬛ AUTUMN TERM ⬛

MUSIC AND REFLECTION

Introduce the music and ask the children to reflect on the stories about presents they have been considering during the last three weeks. What do they consider to be the best gift anyone can be given?

HYMN

The wise may bring their learning *(Come and Praise No. 64)*

PRAYER

What can I give him,
Poor as I am?
If I were a shepherd I would bring a lamb;
If I were a wise man
I would do my part;
Yet what I can I give him –
Give my heart.

Amen

CLOSING REFRAIN

Shalom *(Come and Praise No. 141)*

THE SPRING TERM

Introduction

The Autumn term ended with a look at the giftedness of each person. The Spring term picks up this thread with an exploration into individuality and personal relationships with friends, neighbours and families including the importance of family memories and family roots. The section 'How do you feel today?' offers the chance to examine different feelings. As winter gives way to spring the final theme looks at the experience of loss and pain and relates this to the Christian story of death and resurrection and its implications for everyday life.

THEMES FOR THE SPRING TERM

Theme 1 You and me

Week 1   All about me

Week 2   Our friends

Week 3   Our neighbours

Theme 2 How do you feel today?

Week 1   Feeling happy, feeling sad

Week 2   Fear and courage

Week 3   Feeling angry, feeling peaceful

Theme 3 Families

Week 1   Belonging to a family

Week 2   Family memories

Week 3   Family roots

Theme 4 Losing and finding

Week 1   Loss and pain

Week 2   New beginnings

Week 3   Signs of renewal

SPRING TERM
THEME 1: *You and me*

Week 1
All about me

Week 2
Our friends

Week 3
Our neighbours

Checklist for Hymn Practice

If I were a butterfly *(Junior Praise No. 94 and Come and Sing some more No. 27)*
God knows me *(Come and Praise No. 15)*

With a little help from my friends *(Alleluya, 77 songs for thinking people No. 38)*
Cross over the road *(Come and Praise No. 70)*

When I needed a neighbour *(Come and Praise No. 65)*
Kum ba yah *(Come and Praise No. 68)*

■■■■■■■■ SPRING TERM ■■■■■■■■

THEME 1: Week 1

THEME FOR THE WEEK
All about me

AIM: **To help develop a sense of identity and an awareness of the uniqueness of each person and their value in the sight of God.**

SETTING OUT
Collective worship for the beginning of the week

 ## GATHERING

During this time try to make the children aware of the richness of differences between all individuals.

Compare: Physical differences . . . heights, colour of eyes, types of hair; personalities and preferences . . . who likes being quiet, noisy, alone, in a crowd? Skills . . . who can skip backwards, balance two books on their head, recite a poem, head a football, play a musical instrument? Try to choose examples which may be demonstrated.

 ## LISTENING

YOU AND ME

Who am I and what can I do?
And how is it that you are you?
Is it simply the wave in your hair,
Or the way you swing your arms in the air?

I can do somersaults brilliantly fast,
But I can't tie a bow in my lace that will last.
You ride your bike with the greatest of ease,
But the sight of a mouse gives you wobbly knees.

I am me and you are you.
What different things we two can do.
It's still a mystery to me,
How I'm not you and you're not me.

SPRING TERM

MUSIC AND REFLECTION

Introduce the music and ask the children to reflect on their individuality and the amazing fact that there is only one person exactly like them in the whole world.

HYMN

If I were a butterfly *(Junior Praise No. 94 and Come and Sing Some More No. 27)*

PRAYER

Thank you God for the life which you have given us and the special place we each have in your world. Help us to rejoice in all the talents and abilities which we have and to use our lives to your glory.

Amen

CLOSING REFRAIN

Shalom *(Come and Praise No. 141)*

TRAVELLING FURTHER

In your worship time try to:

- Develop a sense of the uniqueness of each individual.
- Develop a sense of wonder at the different capabilities each person has.
- Think about all the things they can do with their hands, bodies and minds.
- Develop a sense of self-worth and an appreciation of their own skills and of the abilities of others.

Make a gallery of handprints and or fingerprints and examine how each one is different.

Make a portrait gallery with a self-portrait or photograph of each child, accompanied by a description they have written about themselves describing their physical characteristics, likes and dislikes, skills and interests.

Make a class exhibition entitled 'I can do this with my hands'.
Include as wide a variety of art, craft and music making as possible.

Prepare a display entitled 'I can do this with my body'. The class could work in groups to show skills in dance, gymnastics, sport and athletics.

Make a wordsearch or crossword about different parts of the body: e.g. a wordsearch about the skeleton using all the names of the bones or a crossword about the heart, lungs and blood system.

ON THE HOME STRAIGHT
Collective worship for the end of the week

 GATHERING

Remind the children that they have been thinking about themselves and all they can do.

 LISTENING

This could take the form of a presentation and discussion of work achieved during the week or a display of skills: e.g. a child could talk about how to make a model or a gymnast could give a display.

 MUSIC AND REFLECTION

Introduce the music and ask the children to think of all the things they can do and the ways in which they are unique.

 HYMN

God knows me *(Come and Praise No. 15)*

 PRAYER

We thank you God for creating us and for the wonderful gifts of body and mind which you have given each one of us.
Thank you for all the things which make us unique.
Help us to remember that each one of us is precious in your sight and that you love us all.

Amen

 CLOSING REFRAIN

Shalom *(Come and Praise No. 141)*.

SPRING TERM

THEME 1: Week 2

THEME FOR THE WEEK
Our friends

AIM: **To consider the importance of friends in our lives and what makes a person a good friend.**

SETTING OUT
Collective worship for the beginning of the week

 ## GATHERING

Introduce the idea of friends:

- Who is their best friend?
- How do we choose friends? (Shared interests? Personality? Someone we can trust?)
- What makes a good friend? (Someone who is loyal? Someone who can tell us if we are doing wrong? Someone who will put up with our bad points as well as our good ones?)
- How do we feel if we have no friends?

 ## LISTENING

Read the version of the story of Ruth below or tell the story in your own words.

RUTH THE LOYAL FRIEND

Long, long ago there was a famine in the land of Judah. A man called Elimelech decided to take his wife Naomi and their two sons from Bethlehem, where they lived, to the country of the Moabites because they needed to find food. The family stayed in the strange new country and found food and work.

The two sons grew up there and married two Moabite girls whose names were Orpah and Ruth. After a few years however, Elimelech, the father, died. Then, some years later, both Naomi's sons died and the three women Naomi, Orpah and Ruth were left alone.

Naomi said to her two daughters-in-law, 'I am an old woman now. I left all my friends in Bethlehem and I would like to go back to my own country. Both of you have lived in Moabite country all your lives. You have friends and relatives here and you are young enough to marry again. You stay here and make a new life for yourselves but I am an old woman and all I want is to go back to my own land and my own people.' Then

■ SPRING TERM ■

with many tears Orpah left Naomi. Ruth, however, refused to leave Naomi and insisted on travelling the long journey back to Bethlehem with her.

At first Naomi argued and said to Ruth, 'Look your sister Orpah has gone to stay with her family. Why don't you stay too?' But Ruth was determined to stay with Naomi to comfort her and be her friend.

'Dear Naomi do not make me leave you,' said Ruth. 'Where you go I will go, and where you stay I will stay. Your people shall be my people and your God my God. Where you die I will die and there I will be buried. I swear a solemn oath before the Lord your God: nothing but death shall divide us.'

When Naomi saw that Ruth was determined to go with her, she said no more and the two of them went on until they came to Bethlehem.

(Adapted from the story in Ruth 1)

MUSIC AND REFLECTION

Introduce the music and ask the children to reflect on how Ruth was a good friend to Naomi and to think about times in their lives when their friends have been kind and loyal to them.

HYMN

With a little help from my friends *(Alleluya, 77 songs for thinking people No. 38)*

PRAYER

Lord Jesus thank you for our friends.
Thank you for all the times when our friends help us.
Thank you for friends who share both our happiness and our sadness.
Help us to be good friends to those around us.

Amen

CLOSING REFRAIN

Shalom *(Come and Praise No. 141)*

SPRING TERM

TRAVELLING FURTHER
In your worship time try to:

- Reflect on the nature of friendship.
- Define the qualities of a good friend.
- Reflect on how friends can help by comfort, encouragement or criticism.
- Become aware of the picture of God as a friend, as portrayed by Jesus.

Tell in your own words or read from a children's Bible the story of the paralysed man and his four friends (Mark 2. 1 – 12). Ask the children to re-tell the story as if they were one of the characters in the story.

Write a class poem entitled 'A friend is. . .' Encourage each child to contribute a line to the poem. Start each line with 'A friend is someone who . . . ' e.g. 'A friend is someone you can tell your secrets to.'

Show the video, or tell the story, *John Brown, Rose and the Midnight Cat* by Jenny Wagner (published by Viking, Kestrel). Video obtainable from Weston Woods, 14 Friday Street, Henley on Thames, Oxfordshire (Customer services telephone 0491 577033). Explore the ideas about friendship in the book. Are there times when friendship can be selfish and exclusive?

Discuss how Jesus chose special friends (disciples) to be with him and share his work. Read or tell the story in Mark 14. 32 – 50 and talk about whether the disciples were good friends in the story. (You may need to put the story in the context of the events of Holy Week.)

SPRING TERM

ON THE HOME STRAIGHT
Collective worship for the end of the week

GATHERING
Share with the children some of their thinking about friendship during the week.

LISTENING
Arrange for the children to tell the story of the four friends and the paralysed man or to read their class poem on 'Friendship'.

MUSIC AND REFLECTION
Introduce the music and ask the children to reflect on what they enjoy about being with friends.

HYMN
Cross over the road *(Come and Praise No. 70)*

PRAYER
For friends with whom we can share a joke.
For friends who can make us laugh and giggle.
For friends who stay around when we are sad.
For friends who will share our deepest fears.
For friends who comfort us when we are miserable.
For friends who are not afraid to tell us we are wrong.
Thanks be to God for friends.

Amen

CLOSING REFRAIN
Shalom *(Come and Praise No. 141)*

SPRING TERM

THEME 1: Week 3

THEME FOR THE WEEK
Our neighbours

AIM: **To help children realize that we are all dependent on each other's care, to help them become aware of all the people who care for them and to explore what it means to be a good neighbour.**

SETTING OUT
Collective worship for the beginning of the week

✦ GATHERING

Ask the children to name all those who help them each day. Try to gather as wide a group of examples as possible – parents, crossing patrol assistants, dinner staff, coach driver, doctors, dentists etc. Explain that in worship time this week we are thinking of all those who care for us and about being good neighbours to each other.

LISTENING

MRS FANSHAW'S NEIGHBOURS

Mrs Fanshaw dragged herself on her side across the kitchen floor and into the hall of her flat on the first level of the tower block. Her ankle was excruciatingly painful and she could not stand. She managed to pull herself up to a sitting position and rubbed her foot gently. 'Stupid woman,' she said to herself, 'now look what a mess you are in.' She had slipped on a wet patch on the lino as she hurried to the front door to catch the milkman. She had shouted out in pain as she fell but the milkman, with all the clattering of bottles, did not hear her. Now there was nothing for it but to wait to see if she could attract the attention of the paper boy. How she wished she had taken the advice of her daughter to have a telephone fitted.

Tim the paper boy was just toiling up the stairs to Mrs Fanshaw's flat. He folded the paper carefully and quietly lifted the letter box. Tim did not like Mrs Fanshaw. Once he had accidentally torn her paper getting it through the letter box and she had run after him shouting and screaming. On another very wet, windy morning he had dropped her paper in the rain and she had complained to the paper shop and refused to pay

SPRING TERM

her bill. The paper shop had docked his wages that week as a punishment. So when he heard her calling out, as he pushed the paper through the door, Tim turned away quickly and began to hurry towards the stairs. At the top he bumped into the postman.

'You're in a hurry,' said George the postman.

'It's Mrs Fanshaw, she's shouting at me again,' said Tim.

The postman listened. 'You're right, she is shouting, but I don't think she is shouting at you. She's shouting for help.' So Tim and George went back to the door of the flat and looked through the letter box. They could see Mrs Fanshaw lying in a heap near the door to the kitchen. She didn't seem to move much when George shouted through the opening. 'We must get some help,' said George. 'You stay here and keep talking to her even though she doesn't answer. I'll go and get some help.' So Tim stayed by the door calling gently to Mrs Fanshaw and trying to comfort her whilst George went to ring for help.

In no time at all the police had arrived and found a way to open the door. Next the ambulance crew arrived and carried Mrs Fanshaw on a stretcher to the waiting ambulance. By that time all the neighbours were alerted to what had happened. They praised Tim for being so alert and they talked about what they should all do to help Mrs Fanshaw when she came out of hospital. How would she be able to manage if she was in plaster and what ought they to do to help?

What do you think they could do?

MUSIC AND REFLECTION

Introduce the music and ask the children to think about the help Mrs Fanshaw would need. Who would be able to help her and how?

HYMN

When I needed a neighbour *(Come and Praise No. 65)*

PRAYER

Lord, we thank you for our good neighbours. We remember those who care for us every day.

Help us to be good friends and neighbours to those around us.

Amen

CLOSING REFRAIN

Shalom *(Come and Praise No. 141)*

TRAVELLING FURTHER

In your worship time try to:

- Develop a sense of our inter-dependence.
- Raise an awareness of the work of all those in the community who help us.
- Find out about the rewards and difficulties of some of the caring jobs in our community.
- Foster a sense of responsibility to those around us.

Make a collage entitled 'People who help us'. Include drawings, or cut outs, of postmen, road sweepers, electricians, nurses, teachers, firemen, policemen etc.

Arrange a visit and, with the class, prepare an interview of someone who works in the community. This could be a health visitor, social worker, policeman etc.

Make a class mobile with the theme 'Who will help us?' On oblong cards write a 'problem' on one side of the card and on the other draw a person who could help e.g. We need clean roads – drawing of a road sweeper.

Make a class game entitled 'Good Neighbours'. This could be in the form of a Snakes and Ladders type board game with snakes for problems e.g. knocked down by car, and ladders for when help comes e.g. ambulance man arrives. Try to include problems where the children could contribute to the solution.

Prepare the story of the Good Samaritan (Luke 10. 30 – 37) as a drama. (*The dramatised Bible*, edited by Michael Perry, published by Marshall Pickering could be a useful aid.)

USEFUL BOOKS

People Who Help Us series (published by Wayland). (Separate books on many service occupations including Ambulance crew, Bus Driver and Lifeboat crew.

SPRING TERM

ON THE HOME STRAIGHT
Collective worship for the end of the week

GATHERING

Remind the children that they have been thinking about being good neighbours. Read Luke 10. 27 – 28: Jesus said 'Love the Lord your God with all your heart, with all your soul, with all your strength, and with all your mind; and your neighbour as yourself'. Explain that Jesus told the following story to explain the way he wanted us to care.

LISTENING

In your own words, or using the drama the children have prepared, tell the story of the Good Samaritan.

MUSIC AND REFLECTION

Introduce the music and ask the children to reflect on the story of the good Samaritan. In what ways can we be good neighbours to those around us?

HYMN

Kum ba yah *(Come and Praise No. 68)*

PRAYER

PRAYER OF ST THERESA

Christ has no body now on earth but yours,
no hands but yours, no feet but yours.
Yours are the feet with which He is to go about doing good.
Yours are the hands with which He is to bless men now.

Amen

CLOSING REFRAIN

Shalom *(Come and Praise No. 141)*

SPRING TERM
THEME 2: *How do you feel today?*

Week 1
Feeling happy, feeling sad

Week 2
Fear and courage

Week 3
Feeling angry, feeling
peaceful

Checklist for Hymn Practice

Guess how I feel? *(Come and Praise No. 89)*
O Lord shout for joy *(Someone's singing Lord No. 4)*

My faith it is an oaken staff *(Come and Praise No. 46)*
Only a boy called David *(Junior Praise No. 190)*

Do not be afraid for I have redeemed you *(Mission Praise No. 115)*
Now be strong *(Junior Praise No. 172)*

The prayer of St Francis *(Come and Praise No. 147)*
Down by the riverside *(Come and Praise No. 142)*

━━━━━━━━━━ **SPRING TERM** ━━━━━━━━━━

THEME 2: Week 1

THEME FOR THE WEEK
Feeling happy, feeling sad

AIM: **To help the children recognize and identify their feelings and to develop ways of coping with them.**

SETTING OUT
Collective worship for the beginning of the week (This will need preparation beforehand.)

Before the Collective Worship ask four children to mime walking into the worship area as if they were either happy, sad, angry or afraid. It is important that other people do not know this.

 ## GATHERING

Ask the spectators to guess the feelings of the four performing the mimes. Can we reecognise how people feel by their movements?
What do we do if we are sad?
Are there ways of helping ourselves feel better when we are sad?

 ## LISTENING

Introduce the following story:

THE BRAVEST MAN IN THE CIRCUS

Coco the clown sat, slumped on the steps of his caravan. The Ringmaster of the circus sat beside him on an up-turned crate.

'Well Coco,' said the Ringmaster, 'how do you feel about performing tonight? Do you think you can make it?' Coco shrugged his shoulders, put his head in his hands and gave a big sigh.

'I don't think I can ever clown again,' he said. 'How can I make other people laugh when all I want to do is cry?'

'We all sympathise with you,' said the Ringmaster. 'When your dog Clippy was knocked down and killed last night it shocked the whole circus community. We all feel as if we have lost a good friend.'

'Clippy was part of my act. The way he ran around the ring with me, jumped through the hoops and barked when I asked him questions. He was almost human. I just can't think of performing without him,' said Coco.

The Ringmaster put his hand on Coco's shoulder and got up. 'Well Coco, it's up to you. We'll understand if you feel you can't go on. Just let me know by this afternoon.'

Just then Melissa, the tight-rope artist, who lived in the caravan next to Coco came out. She was carrying two cups of coffee. She gave one to Coco and sat down beside him. They sat in silence on the caravan steps. 'The audience would miss you tonight Coco. Everyone loves your act especially the children. You manage to get a laugh out of the most miserable person. They roll about when you do that bit trying to balance on a ball and when you try to carry that tray of glasses on your head and trip over they all roar with delight. Everyone loves a clown. I suppose it's because a clown is so . . .' Melissa stopped speaking because Coco had walked away. She watched him wander into the Big Top but did not follow him.

All that morning Coco walked around the circus thinking. The other circus people patted him on the shoulder as they walked by. Some just gave him a hug. In the afternoon Coco sat by the ringside. The juggler left a ham sandwich for him to eat. The acrobats quietly put a large flask of tea and a mug beside him.

That evening, as the crowds began to meander from the town towards the circus, Coco slowly and methodically put on his make-up: the high arched eyebrows and of course the wide red gash of a smile. By the time the circus band was striking up their first chords Coco was ready with the other artists at the entrance to the ring. Suddenly the Ringmaster was announcing 'The Clowns' and Coco was there tumbling and somersaulting, doing all the ridiculous things he had done for years, despite the ache in his heart. At first Coco found that he was doing everything mechanically. He could feel nothing and simply went through his well rehearsed routine. Then, suddenly, as he picked himself up from a series of somersaults, he caught sight of a tiny boy at the ringside rolling with laughter and holding out his arms to Coco in wild delight. Coco heard the laughter of the audience and their applause, as if for the first time. Although he still felt sad, he felt comfort from the laughter and a strange peace and kind of happiness.

When the last act was over the artists came into the ring in the 'The Grand Parade'. Coco was last and as he walked into the spotlight the Ringmaster announced him, 'Coco the clown, the bravest man in the Circus'. There were all his friends: the trapeze artist, the jugglers, the acrobats and the trick cyclists. They stood around him cheering and applauding and Coco then understood how they shared both his sadness and his joy. He dared to believe that, one day, there would be laughter in his heart again.

MUSIC AND REFLECTION

Introduce the music and ask the children to reflect on the story and the feelings of Coco. How did his friends help him to feel better? How did he help himself?

HYMN

Guess how I feel *(Come and Praise No. 89)*

SPRING TERM

PRAYER

Thank you God for being with us whether we feel happy or sad, peaceful or worried. Thank you for the times when we feel happy and help us to be brave and courageous when we feel sad.

Amen

CLOSING REFRAIN

Shalom *(Come and Praise No. 141)*

TRAVELLING FURTHER

In your worship time try to:

- Help the children to recognize their feelings.
- Help the children to identify their feelings.
- Help the children to recognize 'the body language' of themselves and of other people.
- Help the children to develop strategies for dealing with 'negative' feelings.

Make a Gallery of faces showing a variety of feelings. Ask the children to bring photographs, cuttings from newspapers or magazines, or their own drawings or paintings. Give time to look at the gallery and to discuss and identify the feelings displayed.

Make a class joke anthology entitled 'This makes me laugh'.

Make a class anthology entitled 'I feel sad when . . .'

In mime and movement explore together how facial expressions and body language can express the moods of: anger, despair, joy, surprise, disgust, shame, sorrow, boredom, fear, nervousness and sadness.

In discussion share ways of coping with sad feelings. What can a person do to feel more at peace with themselves again?

Collect sayings which are used to cheer people up: 'Keep your chin up', 'Keep smiling', 'Whistle a happy tune', 'Look for the silver lining', Do these sayings help?

USEFUL BOOKS

Health and Friends by Dorothy Baldwin (published by Wayland).
Health and Feelings by Dorothy Baldwin (published by Wayland).

Spring Term

ON THE HOME STRAIGHT
Collective worship for the end of the week

 ## GATHERING

Remind the children of the theme of feelings and ask how they are feeling today. Who is feeling happy, sad, cross or afraid?

 ## LISTENING

Use this time to share comment on the work done during the week. Alternatively prepare beforehand a presentation called 'This makes me laugh'. This could include jokes, stories or poems.

 ## MUSIC AND REFLECTION

Introduce the music and ask the children to think about times when they have felt really happy. What made them happy?

HYMN

O Lord Shout for Joy *(Someone's singing Lord No. 4)*

PRAYER

We thank you God for happy times when we can laugh and smile, when our hearts feel full of joy and love. Help us to share our good feelings with those around us and teach us to ask for help when we are angry, sad or afraid.

Amen

 ## CLOSING REFRAIN

Shalom *(Come and Praise No. 141)*

SPRING TERM

THEME 2: Week 2

THEME FOR THE WEEK
Fear and courage

AIM: **To help children identify their fears and develop ways of coping with them.**

SETTING OUT
Collective worship for the beginning of the week

GATHERING

Tell the children that you are going to read a description of a boy and they are to try to identify his feelings:

Robert was standing at the bottom of the stairs. His hands felt clammy and he could feel his shirt sticking to him. His legs felt as if they were about to collapse beneath him and his stomach was churning over.

How did Robert feel?

LISTENING

Tell the children that you are going to read them a story about a courageous boy.

Long, long ago there was a terrible war between the Philistines and the Israelites. At that time there was an old man, Jesse, who lived near Bethlehem, not far from the scene of the fighting. Three of Jesse's sons were fighting for King Saul of the Israelites but his youngest son, David, had stayed at home to help look after the sheep. One day Jesse said, 'David, I want to know how my sons are. Take these cheeses, loaves of bread and this grain and go to see if your brothers are well and bring me back news'. So, early next morning, David left someone in charge of the sheep and set out as Jesse had asked him.

When he reached the place, where the army camped, David saw the lines of Israelite soldiers on one side of the valley and the Philistines opposite. David found his brothers and while he was talking with them the champion soldier of the Philistines, whose name was Goliath, came out from the ranks and shouted across the valley: 'I am Goliath, the Philistine champion. Choose your man to meet me. If he can kill me in fair fight we will become your slaves but if I prove too strong for him and kill him, then you shall be our slaves and serve us'. When the Israelites saw Goliath they ran from him in fear for not one of them dared to face the giant Goliath.

But David said, 'Who is this Philistine to defy the army of the living God? Surely we need not be afraid, for we fight in the power of the God of Israel.'

Then David's elder brother grew angry and said, 'Who do you think you are, you impudent young rascal. Go home and look after the sheep in the wilderness.' But some of the other soldiers had heard David and took David to King Saul.

David said to the King, 'Do not lose heart sir. I will go and fight this Philistine'.

King Saul answered, 'You cannot go and fight with Goliath. You are only a lad and he has been a fighting man all his life.'

David held his ground and said, 'I am my father's shepherd; when a lion or bear carries off a sheep from the flock, I go after it, attack it, and rescue the victim from it's jaws. I have killed lions and bears. The Lord who saved me from the lions and the bears will save me from this Goliath.'

'Go then,' said King Saul, but first let me give you some armour.'

So David tried on the bronze helmet and a coat of mail, but they were so heavy he could not move. 'I cannot go in this armour,' he said. 'Let me go as I am. I will choose five smooth stones from the brook and take my catapult.'

Then David walked out into the valley a young slim boy armed only with a shepherds sling and a few stones. There was Goliath standing before him, over nine feet tall, wearing a bronze helmet and plate armour and carrying both a sword and a dagger. Goliath looked David up and down and laughed at him in scorn.

David said, 'All the world shall know that there is a God in Israel and that the Lord saves neither by sword nor spear. Today you will see the might of our God.'

Then Goliath started to move towards David but David ran swiftly, took a stone, put it in his sling and, with a swoop of his arm, sent the stone arching through the air towards Goliath. The stone struck the Philistine right in the centre of his forehead and sunk in and Goliath fell to the ground. Then David ran to Goliath and taking his sword, he killed Goliath with a mighty stab.

The Philistines, when they saw that their hero was dead, turned and ran and David returned to King Saul triumphant.

(adapted from 1 Samuel 17)

MUSIC AND REFLECTION

Introduce the music and ask the children to reflect on the story. Who was afraid in the story, who was courageous and how was fear overcome?

HYMN

My faith it is an oaken staff *(Come and Praise No. 46)*
Only a boy called David *(Junior Praise No. 190)*

Spring Term

PRAYER

Lord, we are all afraid sometimes.
Help us to understand our fears.
Help us to encourage each other to face whatever frightens us.
Help us to be bold and brave and may we know the comfort of your promise to be with us always.

Amen

CLOSING REFRAIN

Shalom *(Come and Praise No. 141)*

TRAVELLING FURTHER

In your worship time try to:

- Explore the feelings of fear and identify what makes us feel afraid.
- Look at the strategies of overcoming fear – fight or flight? Are there times when it is not cowardly to run away?
- Look at ways of helping ourselves and others to be more courageous.
- Discuss whether courage can exist without fear.

Make a class book or picture entitled 'Fears - Real or Imaginary'. Give the children time to discuss what makes them frightened.

In groups, share stories about 'The time I was most scared was when . . .'

Look at the following stories of fear and consider what it was that made the people concerned afraid? Where did they turn for help?

- The disciples are afraid on the lake (Matthew 8. 23 – 28).
- The Christian Ananias visits Saul the persecutor of Christians (Acts 9. 10 – 19).
- Jesus faces fear in the Garden of Gethsemene (Matthew 26. 36 – 46)

Using the starting sentence, 'Whenever I feel afraid . . .' gather ideas for helping to face fear. Whistling in the dark? Singing? Sharing fears with a friend? Finding out more about whatever it is frightens us? (You might like to use the music 'I Whistle a Happy Tune' from *The King and I,* Rodgers and Hammerstein IMP 03512 as a starter for discussion.) This could be a valuable opportunity to discuss the bullying issue.

Use the story of David and Goliath or other stories of 'giant -killers' as the basis for exploring the feelings of fear and courage through drama.

SPRING TERM

USEFUL BOOKS ABOUT FEARS

There's a nightmare in my cupboard by Mercer Mayer (published by Dent). *The owl who was afraid of the dark* by Jill Tomlinson (published by Methuen) Young Puffin paperback.

ON THE HOME STRAIGHT

Collective worship for the end of the week

GATHERING

Remind the children that they have been exploring the feelings of fear.

LISTENING

Use this time to share some of the work done during the week, or, you may prefer to tell the story of Christ bringing reassurance to the frightened disciples (Matthew 8. 23 – 28).

MUSIC AND REFLECTION

Introduce the music and ask the children to think of ways they can become more courageous and help others to be brave too.

HYMN

Do not be afraid for I have redeemed you *(Mission Praise No. 115)* Now be Strong *(Junior Praise No. 172)*

PRAYER

Lord, we thank you that you are with us when we feel brave and when we are afraid.

Thank you for the courage which comes from knowing that you love and care for us all through our lives.

Amen

CLOSING REFRAIN

Shalom *(Come and Praise No. 141)*

SPRING TERM

THEME 2: Week 3

THEME FOR THE WEEK
Feeling angry, feeling peaceful

AIM: **To help the children to identify the feeling of anger and to work out acceptable ways of dealing with it. To help children to discover what helps them to feel peaceable.**

SETTING OUT
Collective worship for the beginning of the week

GATHERING
Discuss the experience of anger?

● How does it feel to be really angry?
● What happens to people's bodies when they feel angry?
● Do the children enjoy the feeling of anger or does it make them feel uncomfortable?
● How do they feel when someone is angry with them?

LISTENING

ADAM AND THE ANGRY BALL

Adam was feeling cross, very cross, furious. In fact he was angry. He had wanted to finish making a model but his Mum made him clear it up and get ready for bed. 'It's not fair', Adam complained. 'I wanted to finish painting the wings on the aeroplane.'

'But I want you to be ready for bed before Gran arrives. Dad and I are going out to see friends tonight and you know Gran will be here for the evening.'

Adam still grumbled. He stamped up the stairs and took ages in the bath until Mum came back and shouted at him to hurry up. Then, he deliberately splashed water all over the floor and left the bathroom in a dreadful mess. He slung himself into bed and pulled the duvet cover over his head. He didn't even answer Mum and Dad when they came to say goodbye before they left.

Then he heard Gran come into the bedroom. She sat on the end of the bed but she didn't say anything. At last Adam stuck his head out from under the duvet. 'Feeling mad with life?' enquired Gran. Adam found himself telling Gran all about his day: how he had lost at football, been pushed over in the playground, broken his best pen, and then had to go to bed when he wanted to finish his model.

Gran listened in silence. 'So what did you do to make things feel better?' Gran asked.

'I stamped up the stairs, that felt good,' said Adam. 'Then I made a dreadful mess in the bathroom and left it all for Mum to clear up'.

'Did that help?' asked Gran.

Adam thought about it. 'Not really, I felt a bit mean making extra work for Mum, when she wanted to go out, and I wish I had said goodbye.'

'How do you feel when you are angry?' Gran asked.

'I feel . . . I feel . . . as if I want to really kick everyone very hard.'

'But supposing you did kick someone . . . Mum . . . Dad . . . the cat . . . what would you feel then?' asked Gran.

'I would be really ashamed of myself and I would get into trouble too,' Adam said.

'So what could you kick that wouldn't hurt anyone but would make you feel better?'

'I could kick my red football against the garden wall or I could punch my pillow really hard, that wouldn't hurt anyone and it might make me feel better,' Adam agreed.

'Do you feel better now?' asked Gran.

Adam smiled, 'I feel better for telling you why I felt angry'.

'So that's something else that you could do. You could share your anger by talking it over with someone else. Perhaps if you did that you might not even want to kick at all.'

Adam laughed, 'Maybe, but until then I shall call my red ball an angry ball and, when I feel life is unfair, I shall kick it up and down the garden until I feel less angry.'

'Sounds a good idea to me,' said Gran, and she gave Adam a hug.

MUSIC AND REFLECTION

Introduce the music and ask the children to reflect on what makes them feel angry and what helps them to feel at peace.

HYMN

The prayer of St Francis *(Come and Praise No. 147)*

PRAYER

Help us to be channels of peace.
When we feel angry help us to find ways to become peaceful again.
When we feel hatred help us to be loving.
When there has been misunderstanding help us to forgive each other.

Amen

CLOSING REFRAIN

Shalom *(Come and Praise No. 141)*

TRAVELLING FURTHER

In your worship time try to:

- Help children to recognize what makes them feel angry and what helps them to return to peacefulness.
- Help children to recognize what makes other people angry.
- Help children to find acceptable ways of expressing anger.
- Explore ways of feeling at peace with oneself and others.

In pairs devise a one minute dance drama to express anger. You may like to include percussion.

In small groups devise a dance to the words and music of Peace is flowing like a River *(Come and Praise No. 144)*

Paint a picture entitled 'Anger'.

Make a class book entitled 'Peace'. In pictures and writing describe what makes them feel at peace with themselves and others; e.g. I feel at peace when I go for a long walk with the dog . . . I feel at peace when I have a long warm bath . . .

Examine the story of Cain and Abel (Genesis 4. 3 – 16).
Was Cain's anger justified and his action acceptable?

ON THE HOME STRAIGHT

Collective worship for the end of the week

 ### GATHERING

And now my friends . . . mend your ways, take our appeal to heart; agree with one another; live in peace; and the God of love and peace will be with you.

(2 Corinthians 13. 11 – 13)

 ### LISTENING

Use this time to share some of the class work. This could be the dance or drama or presenting parts of the 'Peace' book.

SPRING TERM

 MUSIC AND REFLECTION

Introduce the music and ask the children to reflect on how they can bring peace to those around them.

 HYMN

Down by the riverside *(Come and Praise No. 142)*

 PRAYER

A CELTIC BLESSING

Deep peace of the running wave to you.
Deep peace of the flowing air to you.
Deep peace of the quiet earth to you.
Deep peace of the shining stars to you.
Deep peace of the son of peace to you.

Amen

From *Carmina Gadelica*
Traditional Celtic rune collected by Alexander Carmichael

 CLOSING REFRAIN

Shalom *(Come and Praise No. 141)*

SPRING TERM
THEME 3: *Families*

Week 1
Belonging to a family

Week 2
Family memories

Week 3
Family roots

Checklist for Hymn Practice

Magic penny *(Alleluya, 77 songs for thinking people No. 10)*
Father I place into your hands *(Junior Praise No. 42)*

By the waters of Babylon *(Alleluya, 77 songs for thinking people No. 68)*
Praise to the Lord *(Come and Praise No. 34)*

Father we love you *(Junior Praise No. 45)*
How did Moses cross the Red Sea? *(Junior Praise No. 83)*

■ SPRING TERM ■

THEME 3: Week 1

THEME FOR THE WEEK
Belonging to a family

AIM: To help the children explore what belonging to a family involves.

SETTING OUT
Collective worship for the beginning of the week

 GATHERING

Introduce the theme of families:

- Who belongs to their family?
- What does belonging to a family mean to them (shelter, security, friendship, feeling safe)?
- What do they enjoy about belonging to their family (a sense of belonging, feeling at home)?
- Are there disadvantages in belonging to a family (rules about behaviour, sharing toys, bedrooms and television)?

 LISTENING

Simon and Amanda leaned over the balcony outside their flat. 'I can see Mum coming now,' said Simon.

Mrs Barnet struggled up the stairs her arms full of shopping. 'Sorry I'm a bit late. I missed the bus from work and then there was a long queue at the supermarket. I could do with a cup of tea.'

Amanda took the shopping from her mother's arms and Mrs Barnet opened the front door. Whilst his mother put the shopping away Simon put on the kettle for a cup of tea and Amanda started to lay the table. 'That's a real help,' said Mrs Barnet. 'I've had such a busy day and I'm really grateful to you.'

'My day has been awful,' said Amanda. 'I couldn't understand the maths and then I messed up a model I've been working at for weeks.'

'Poor old Amanda,' said Mum, putting her arms around her shoulder. 'Perhaps I could give you a hand with the maths and maybe you can put the model right tomorrow.

Spring Term

What kind of a day did you have Simon?'

'Mr Groves said he's really pleased with the way I'm improving at football,' said Simon, 'he even said that I might get in the school team if I work hard.'

'That's great,' said Amanda. 'It's really hard to get a place in the team.' They chatted as they prepared their meal and shared the events of the day as they ate together.

When they had finished Simon pushed his chair back. 'I'm going out to practise football in the square,' he said.

'Hang on,' said Amanda. 'It's your turn to do the washing up.'

'It will be dark soon and I must practise if I want to get in the team. Can't you do it tonight?'

'I don't feel like it and anyway there's my favourite programme on television.'

'But it's my turn to choose which programme to watch,' said Simon crossly. Before they realised it, they were in the middle of a dreadful argument. Amanda pushed Simon who slipped, fell against the table and sent a plate crashing to the floor.

'That's enough,' shouted Mrs Barnet. 'I will do the washing up on my own. You're no help if you squabble and fight like this anyway, and neither of you will watch the television. You can go to bed early instead.'

In their bedroom Simon and Amanda lay with their backs to each other in silence. The bedroom door opened softly and Mrs Barnet stood there. 'I'm sorry about the argument,' she said. 'You had both been so good and helpful getting tea. I could have offered to wash up tonight instead of losing my temper. I guess I was just a bit tired.'

'I'm sorry too,' said Amanda. 'I could easily have swapped turns with Simon.'

'There wasn't a programme on the television which I wanted to watch anyway. I was just being awkward,' said Simon.

'I thought sharing cups of cocoa together might help us to be friends again,' said Mrs Barnet as she put a tray of drinks on the bedside table.

MUSIC AND REFLECTION

Ask the children to think about the story. What actions had helped the family to live happily together and what had made for disagreement?

HYMN

Magic Penny *(Alleluya, 77 songs for thinking people No. 10)*

PRAYER

Lord we thank you for our families.
Help us to love one another,
to see the needs of others and be quick to offer help.
Make us ready to forgive and generous enough to ask forgiveness.

Amen

CLOSING REFRAIN

Shalom *(Come and Praise No. 141)*

TRAVELLING FURTHER

In your worship time try to:

- Reflect on the good things about living in a family.
- Reflect on the difficulties of living in a family.
- Understand the need for sharing, caring and forgiving.

Ask each child to draw a picture of their family. Be sensitive to different family structures. Use the drawings as a stimulus for conversation about belonging to a family.

Talk about the place of sharing, caring and forgiving in family life. Ask the children to relate examples of sharing, caring and forgiving and to discuss how they felt.

Design a shield for your family. Try to see that every member is represented on the shield. Alternatively think of symbols which represent what the family means; e.g a flame to represent warmth, a hand to represent care etc.

Write a story entitled 'My idea of a happy family'.

Discuss the place of rules in family life. Are rules necessary?
What rules would you make for your family?

Examine the commandments which God gave to Israel (Exodus 20. 1 – 17). Are they good rules by which to live your life?

ON THE HOME STRAIGHT

Collective worship for the end of the week

 ## GATHERING

Remind the children that they have been thinking about family life.

 ## LISTENING

Use this time to show the art work about families or read the stories about 'My idea of a happy family'.

SPRING TERM

MUSIC AND REFLECTION

Introduce the music and ask the children to think of ways they can help their families to be places of peace and happiness.

HYMN

Father I place into your hands *(Junior Praise No. 42)*

PRAYER

Lord, bless all our families.
Thank you for the laughter and happiness we share.
Thank you for times when we manage to forgive each other and make fresh starts.
Thank you for those who share our sadnesses and disappointments.
Bless our homes and help us to make them places of love and care.

Amen

CLOSING REFRAIN

Shalom *(Come and Praise No. 141)*

SPRING TERM

THEME 3: Week 2

THEME FOR THE WEEK
Family memories

AIM: **To help children to understand the place of memories and tradition in family life and in religious custom.**

SETTING OUT
Collective worship for the beginning of the week

 GATHERING

Remind the children that they are thinking about families and family memories.

- Do they remember a special family outing or family event?
- Can they remember an event which made all the family laugh?

 LISTENING

A MEMORABLE DAY OUT

Uncle Bill came to visit the family once every year in the summer. Every year he would insist on taking the whole family, Mum, Dad, Laura and Darren out for what he called his treat. One year they had all visited London. Another time it had been a day at the seaside. That year Uncle had collected them very early to go to a Theme Park. They had looked forward to this with tremendous excitement but somehow everything seemed to go wrong.

To start with Uncle's car played up and they had to call out the rescue service which took ages. Then, just as they had got going again, Laura had been violently sick. To make matters worse when they arrived at the Theme Park they had to queue for nearly an hour to get in and, just as they had bought their tickets, it began to rain. They had a few turns on a couple of rides but by then the rain had become heavier and the wind was so strong that they could hardly walk straight. They found a shelter near an ornamental lake and decided to eat their packed lunch and then to go home. Everyone felt cold, miserable and terribly disappointed.

Spring Term

Uncle Bill finished his sandwiches first and announced that he would take Laura and Darren to the shop. At least they could buy a souvenir of the day. They made their way along the edge of the lake. Outside the shop a man was selling helium filled balloons. He was holding about twenty of them and they were all blowing wildly in the wind. The balloons were all different colours and had 'Have a Nice Day' printed on the side. Laura decided to have a red one and the man was just disentangling it from the bunch when the wind caught it and pulled it away. 'My balloon!' Laura shouted, and Uncle Bill, without thinking, rushed backwards and jumped to try to catch it.

There was a terrible splash. Laura and Darren turned to see Uncle Bill floundering in the ornamental lake, with water pouring off his hair and ducks wildly quacking in alarm all around him. He was hanging on to Laura's balloon.

Suddenly, Mum and Dad, the shop manager, the balloon man and a whole crowd of other visitors were standing around. Uncle Bill struggled to his feet, waved and gave an elaborate bow. 'Have a nice day,' he called. Then everyone started laughing. They laughed and laughed. The manager of the shop ordered hot drinks for everyone and the balloon man gave all the children a free balloon. They all agreed it would be remembered as the funniest day out ever.

MUSIC AND REFLECTION

Introduce the music and ask the children to think of a favourite family memory and to give thanks for what they enjoyed.

HYMN

By the waters of Babylon *(Alleluya, 77 songs for thinking people No. 68)* Explain that this song is based on a psalm sung by the Jewish people when they were slaves in Babylon remembering their homeland of Zion.

PRAYER

Thank you for the gift of memory:
Memories which help us to understand our past.
Memories which help us to understand those around us.
Memories which bind us together in love for one another.

Amen

CLOSING REFRAIN

Shalom *(Come and Praise No. 141)*

TRAVELLING FURTHER

In your worship time try to:

- Explore family memories.
- Look at the place of memory in religious tradition e.g. the Passover meal, the Last Supper.
- Examine the importance of shared memories in binding people together.

Make a class picture entitled 'Memories'. This could include pictures, newspaper cuttings, postcards and photographs.

'Memory Stories': ask the children to relate their happiest or saddest family memory.

Invite an older member of the community to relate family memories.

Look at the Jewish festival of Passover. What event was it remembering?

Read the story of the Last Supper (1 Corinthians 11. 23 – 26). What do the children think Jesus wanted his disciples to remember about him?

USEFUL BOOKS

Sam's Passover by Lynne Hannigan (published by A & C Black).
Judaism by M Domnitz, Religions of the World series (published by Wayland).
Passover by Lynne Scholefield (published by The Religious and Moral Education Press).
Holy Week by Norma Fairbairn and Jack Priestley (published by The Religious and Moral Education Press).

SPRING TERM

ON THE HOME STRAIGHT
Collective worship for the end of the week

 ## GATHERING

Share some of the memories of the children's families.

 ## LISTENING

This time could be used to present some work about the Passover or the Last Supper or you may prefer to use the following poem.

MEMORIES

'I remember' said Grandad,
As he sat me on his knee.
'I remember summer days . . .
Long ago . . .'
And his eyes became misty.

'I remember,' said Mother,
'Summer days beside the sea.
I remember the sandcastles and . . .'
She passed Grandfather his tea.

'I remember,' said Uncle Jim,
As he looked at the fire's high flames.
'I remember the shouting and the arguments –
And the games . . .'

And then they were all silent
As if lost in their memory.
'I remember . . .' I began,
What is the memory of me?

 ## MUSIC AND REFLECTION

Introduce the music and ask the children to focus their attention on a happy family memory and to think about it in detail.

SPRING TERM

HYMN

Praise to the Lord *(Come and Praise No. 34)*

PRAYER

Thank you God for all the memories we can share together.
Thank you for the happy memories of laughter and joy.
Thank you that we can remember when we have faced difficulties and had strength to overcome our problems.
May we learn from the successes and failures of our past and face each new day with fresh hope and courage.

CLOSING REFRAIN

Shalom *(Come and Praise No. 141)*

SPRING TERM

THEME 3: Week 3

THEME FOR THE WEEK
Family roots

AIM: To help the children develop an understanding of the history of their own family and an awareness of the history of religious families.

SETTING OUT
Collective worship for the beginning of the week (This will need preparation beforehand.)

 ## GATHERING

Remind children of the theme of families and how they have been thinking about family memories.

- How much do they know about the past of their families?
- Where did their parents live as children?
- How far can they trace their family in history?

 ## LISTENING

This may need preparing some weeks beforehand

Arrange for children or staff members to bring an artifact, photograph or other memento and to talk about it for a minute; e.g. this is a medal won by my uncle George in the second world war. This is the wedding veil worn by my auntie at her wedding in 1960. What is known of these relatives?

 ## MUSIC AND REFLECTION

Introduce the music and ask the children to reflect on their families and what they know of them.

 ## HYMN

Father we love you *(Junior Praise No. 45)*

■ SPRING TERM ■

PRAYER
God you are the God of our past since time began.
Thank you for being with us throughout history and for evermore.

Amen

↖↑↗ CLOSING REFRAIN
↙↓↘ Shalom *(Come and Praise No. 141)*

TRAVELLING FURTHER
In your worship time try to:

- Help the children to feel a sense of the history of their family.
- Begin to find out about the foundation people of major religious groups.
- Begin to explore the place of traditions in our lives.

Make a class book of grandparents. Ask each child to draw a grandparent and write something about them.

Introduce the idea of a family tree and ask each child to trace their own family tree as far as possible. Make a class book of family trees.

Read the story of Moses in the Bulrushes (Exodus 2. 1 – 10), Moses and the Burning Bush (Exodus 2. 23 – 25: 3. 1 – 4, 18) or Moses and the escape through the Red Sea (Exodus chapters 14 – 15). *There are many children's versions of these stories.* Explain how Moses was a major figure for the family of Israel. You may like to use one of these stories as the basis for a class drama.

Read the story of the calling of the Disciples. Discuss how these people became the founder members of the Christian Family (Matthew 4. 18 – 22; 9.9). Find out the names of the twelve disciples, (Matthew 10. 1 – 4).

Discuss the meaning of tradition. Have the children got traditions in their families? (Hanging up stockings at Christmas). Are there religious traditions? (hot cross buns on Good Friday, Easter Eggs). Why are traditions important?

ON THE HOME STRAIGHT
Collective worship for the end of the week

 GATHERING

Remind the children of the theme of family roots.

 LISTENING

Use this time to read or act out one of the stories of Moses, a major figure in the family history of the Israelites.

 MUSIC AND REFLECTION

Introduce the music and ask the children to give thanks for all we can learn from stories of the past.

 HYMN

How did Moses cross the Red Sea? *(Junior Praise No. 83)*

 PRAYER

Father of all families, thank you for our family roots and the stories we know about our families. Help us to discover what we can learn from our past.

Amen

 CLOSING REFRAIN

Shalom *(Come and Praise No. 141)*

SPRING TERM
THEME 4: *Losing and finding*

Week 1
Loss and pain

Week 2
New beginnings

Week 3
Signs of renewal

Checklist for Hymn Practice

Jesus, good above all other *(Come and Praise No. 23)*
I cannot tell *(Mission Praise No. 83)*
My song is love unknown *(Mission Praise No. 160)*
There is a green hill *(Junior Praise No. 245)*

All in an Easter Garden *(Come and Praise No. 130)*
Now the green blade riseth *(Come and Praise No. 131)*
Yours be the glory *(Junior Praise No. 299)*

From the darkness came light *(Come and Praise No. 29)*
The Re-cycling song available from Christian Aid, PO Box 100, London SE1 7RT.
O Lord, all the world belongs to you *(Come and Praise No. 39)*

━━━━━ **SPRING TERM** ━━━━━

THEME 4: Week 1

THEME FOR THE WEEK
Loss and pain

AIM: **To explore the experiences of pain and loss and to examine the accounts of the betrayal and crucifixion of Christ.**

SETTING OUT

Collective worship for the beginning of the week

 ## GATHERING

Ask the children if they have ever lost anything they really valued? (e.g. a special toy or book). What other losses have they experienced? (Loss of friendship, loss of status, loss of face).

Explain that this is the time of year when Christians remember when Jesus seemed to lose everything – friends, followers and even his life.

LISTENING

Read the following story.

THE LOSS OF JUDAS

Judas stopped, breathless, and leant against a wall hidden by shadows. He had not stopped running since he had left Jesus and the rest of the disciples at the Passover meal. He had careered through the back streets of Jerusalem and knew he was near the house of the High Priest. He trembled at the thought of what he planned to do.

Turning a corner he saw the house and with a backward glance, to check no-one was around, he slipped inside. He gave his name to a servant and was ushered into a room where the High Priest was sitting together with some of the most powerful people in Jerusalem. Judas knew that the High Priests disliked Jesus. They had been trying to capture Jesus but they could never find an opportunity to arrest him secretly. Since Jesus had such a large following of people they were afraid of creating a riot if they took him prisoner in the daytime. Now Judas Iscariot, a close friend of Jesus, stood before them offering them a plan.

'I promise you, I know where he will be tonight,' said Judas. 'He and his disciples will have gone across the Kidron ravine into the garden of Gethsemane. I know the

---

place. Give me some men and weapons and I promise you Jesus will be in your hands tonight.'

The High Priest looked suspicious. 'It is dark in that garden amongst the olive trees. How will we know which person is Jesus. We could end up arresting someone else. You will have to give us a sign.' Judas looked furtive. Even though he felt in his deepest heart that Jesus knew what he was up to, he had hoped to keep in the shadows and remain unrecognized by the rest of the disciples.

The High Priest was insistent. 'When we get to the garden we will hide in the trees. You must step out ahead of us and greet Jesus. Give him a kiss of greeting and say "Master". That way we will know for sure which is the man.'

Judas turned away. This was not how he had planned it. His heart beat furiously and his mind felt confused. Perhaps, if he asked them for money, they might refuse and the plan could be altered. Was this what he intended? Judas played for time. 'How much would you pay me?' he asked. He heard the tinkle of silver on the table beside him.

'Thirty pieces of silver, that is our offer,' said the High Priest with a smirk.

'It is agreed,' Judas said.

In a matter of moments the High Priest had organised a crowd of men armed with swords and spears. In the dark, and with Judas at the head, they set out for the garden. As they moved stealthily amongst the olive trees Judas suddenly held up his hand. He could see Jesus talking with the disciples in the shadows just ahead of them.

'There they are,' said the High Priest. 'Remember the sign Judas'.

So Judas stepped forward and greeted Jesus. 'Master,' he said, and he gave Jesus a kiss. Then all was noise and confusion. The soldiers sprung out from the darkness and seized Jesus. Holding him fast, they led him away to the house of the High Priest for trial.

All that night Judas thought about what he had done. He wondered what had possessed him in the darkness of that Thursday evening. Why had he done it? Hadn't Jesus been the best friend he had ever had? Hadn't Jesus shown him a new way of living?

At first light Judas put the thirty pieces of silver in a bag and re-traced his steps to the house of the High Priest. 'What I did was wrong,' Judas said. 'Here take back the money.'

'Your feelings are no concern of ours,' said the High Priest. 'Jesus has already been condemned to death. He is even now before Pilate the Roman governor'.

'But I have brought an innocent man to his death,' cried Judas in remorse.

'That's your affair,' said the priests and they showed Judas the door.

Judas stood stunned in the street. He flung the silver coins at the entrance of the temple and then, as the sun rose on the Friday morning, Judas once more began to run through the streets of Jerusalem. Judas knew then what he had lost.

MUSIC AND REFLECTION

Introduce the music and ask the children to imagine themselves as one of the people in the story: Jesus, Judas, one of the disciples. What was their experience?

HYMN

Jesus, good above all other *(Come and Praise No. 23)*
I cannot tell *(Mission Praise No. 83)*

 PRAYER

Lord, sometimes we lose our way and do things we regret.
Sometimes we betray our friends.
Sometimes we hurt those we love most of all.
Help us to feel your love and care, even when we feel ourselves to be unlovable.

Amen

 CLOSING REFRAIN

Shalom *(Come and Praise No. 141)*

TRAVELLING FURTHER

In your worship time try to:

- Explore the experiences and feelings surrounding loss.
- Identify experiences of betrayal in the children's experience.
- Enter imaginatively into the stories surrounding the arrest and betrayal of Jesus.
- Read and act out the story of Peter's denial (Luke 22. 54 – 62).

Read, or act out, the story of the trial before Pilate (Luke 23. 1 – 5, 13 – 25). Discuss how being part of a crowd, or having to make a decision in front of a crowd, might change people's behaviour.

In discussion explore experiences of loss. This might include losing possessions, friendship or loss through death.

Read together the story *Dogger* by Shirley Hughes (published by Collins Picture Lion paperback) or *Badger's Parting Gifts* by Susan Varley (published by Collins Picture Lions).

ON THE HOME STRAIGHT
Collective worship for the end of the week

 ### GATHERING

Share with each other some of the work about loss discussed during the week. Explain that the story you are going to tell is the story of the death of Jesus.

 ### LISTENING

Using a version from a children's Bible, tell the story of the crucifixion.

 ### MUSIC AND REFLECTION

Introduce the music and ask the children to reflect on how Jesus behaved when faced with betrayal, pain and loss.

 ### HYMN

My song is Love Unknown *(Mission Praise No. 160)*
There is a green hill *(Junior Praise No. 245)*

 ### PRAYER

Lord, we remember how Jesus died on the cross.
We remember how he comforted the prisoner dying beside him.
We remember how he asked God's forgiveness for those who were hurting him.
We remember how he experienced pain and loneliness.
We remember how he trusted himself into God's loving care.
When we feel lonely, afraid or in pain, help us to be loving and trusting too.

Amen

 ### CLOSING REFRAIN

Shalom *(Come and Praise No. 141)*

THEME 4: Week 2

THEME FOR THE WEEK
New beginnings

AIM: To explore experiences of new beginnings and fresh starts and to familiarize the children with the Christian stories of resurrection.

SETTING OUT
Collective worship for the beginning of the week

 ## GATHERING

Share with the children thoughts about the experiences of being given a fresh start or a new opportunity:

- What is it like when you start a new book or a clean sheet of paper?
- What is it like when you make friends again after an argument?
- What is it like when you awake from a nightmare and discover a new day with all its opportunities?
- Ask the children to think about how the disciples must have felt after Jesus had died. Discuss how the disciples thought that there would never be a fresh start for them again.

 ## LISTENING

Read the following story to the children:

Early on Sunday morning, whilst it was still dark, Mary Magdalene got up and prepared some sweet smelling oils. She wanted to find the body of Jesus and to anoint it. She knew that Joseph of Arimathaea, a respected member of the community, had bravely gone to Pilate and begged permission to bury the body of Jesus in a garden tomb, cut out of the rock. Joseph had wrapped the body of Jesus in a linen sheet, laid him in the tomb and rolled a stone against the entrance. It was just after sunrise as Mary made her way to the tomb. As she walked, she wondered how she could possibly move the heavy stone from across the entrance. When she drew nearer, she saw that the stone had already been moved. Mary was horrified and, at once, ran to find Simon Peter and the other disciple whom Jesus loved. 'Oh come quickly,' Mary cried. 'They have taken the Lord out of his tomb and we do not know where they have laid him.'

SPRING TERM

Peter and the other disciple set out at once and ran all the way to the tomb. The other disciple reached the tomb first and, peering in, saw the linen sheet lying folded. Then Simon Peter arrived and both the disciples went into the tomb. They saw the sheet and the bandage folded up but there was no sign of the body. Then both the disciples went home.

Mary stood, weeping, outside the tomb. As she wept, she peered into the tomb and there she saw two angels in white, one at the head and one at the feet where the body of Jesus had been. They said to her, 'Why are you weeping?'

Mary answered, 'They have taken my Lord away and I do not know where they have laid him.' Then she turned around and Jesus was standing there but she did not recognize him.

Jesus said to Mary, 'Who is it you are looking for?'

Mary thinking Jesus was the gardener said, 'Sir, if you, have removed Jesus from the tomb, tell me where you have laid him and I will take him away.'

Jesus said 'Mary'. Mary turned in amazement and said, 'It is the Lord.'

'Go to my friends and tell them what you have seen,' said Jesus.

Mary ran and found the disciples and told them, 'I have seen the Lord. He is risen indeed.'

MUSIC AND REFLECTION

Introduce the music and ask the children to reflect on the story. Which part do they find most vivid?

HYMN

All in an Easter Garden (*Come and Praise No. 130*)
Yours be the glory (*Junior Praise No. 299*)
Now the green blade riseth (*Come and Praise No. 131*)

PRAYER

Thank you God for the opportunities of new life which you give us every day. Thank you for the chances we have to make new starts and fresh beginnings.
Thank you for the hope you bring of love conquering death.
Thank you for the message and joy of Easter.

Amen

CLOSING REFRAIN

Shalom (*Come and Praise No. 141*)

TRAVELLING FURTHER

In your worship time try to:

- Share experiences of new beginnings and fresh starts.
- Think about symbols of new life.
- Recognize signs of resurrection in the natural world.
- Look at myths and legends of resurrection from all traditions; e.g. the tale of Persephone and the coming of Spring or the legend of the Phoenix.

Read the story of the friends on the road to Emmaus (Luke 24. 13 – 35).

Read again the resurrection account (John 20. 1 – 18) and make an Easter garden, complete with the tomb and the stone rolled away.

Make a 'Resurrection Tree': firmly plant a bare twiggy branch in a flower pot and hang symbols of new life from the spurs. The symbols can be drawn and cut out of card and could include: eggs, rabbits, chicks, lambs, butterflies, spring flowers.

Make an Easter card illustrating a resurrection story or showing a symbol of resurrection.

Tell the legend of Persephone and the coming of spring.

USEFUL BOOKS

Orchard Book of Greek Myths by Geraldine McCaughrean (published by Orchard).
Legends of Ancient Greece by James Reeves (published by Piper).

ON THE HOME STRAIGHT
Collective worship for the end of the week

 GATHERING

Remind the children of the theme of new beginnings.

 LISTENING

Use this time to share some of the work achieved during the week. The children may like to display and talk about their gardens, cards or resurrection trees. Alternatively read another account of the resurrection; e.g. The Road to Emmaus (Luke 24. 13 – 35) or Jesus appears to the disciples on the shore (John 21. 1 – 14).

 MUSIC AND REFLECTION

Introduce the music and ask the children to reflect on signs of new life around them and to give thanks for it.

 HYMN

From the darkness came light *(Come and Praise No. 29)*

 PRAYER

For the wonder of each new day with its hope of new beginnings.
For the promise of spring and new life in nature.
For the hope of courage and love overcoming despair and hatred,
And for the good news of Easter,
We give thanks and praise.

Amen

 CLOSING REFRAIN

Shalom *(Come and Praise No. 141)*

SPRING TERM

THEME 4: Week 3

THEME FOR THE WEEK
Signs of renewal

AIM: **To help the children find practical ways of living out their ideas of resurrection and to help them make links between their beliefs and their behaviour.**

SETTING OUT
Collective worship for the beginning of the week (This will need preparation beforehand.)

GATHERING

Remind the children that they have been thinking about resurrection and signs of resurrection, including the signs of spring.

- Are there special jobs which are done in the spring?
- Do they know what 'Spring Cleaning' is?
- What happens to the things which are turned out at spring cleaning.
- Are there things which we throw away everyday?

LISTENING

Prepare in advance a waste bin or refuse sack containing a selection of rubbish. This could include: empty cans, empty cereal packets, old envelopes, glass or plastic bottles, vegetable peelings wrapped up in paper, empty margarine tubs.

Ask the children to take something from the sack: Ask them, is it waste? Could it be resurrected by re-cycling or using in a different way?

MUSIC AND REFLECTION

Introduce the music and ask the children to think of the things they throw away. How could these items be given new life?

HYMN

The Re-cycling Song *(available from Christian Aid, PO Box 100, London, SE1 7RT)*

SPRING TERM

PRAYER

Lord, the earth is full of the beauty of your creation.
Help us to use all your gifts with care, so that we do not waste the valuable resources given to us.

Amen

CLOSING REFRAIN

Shalom *(Come and Praise No. 141)*

TRAVELLING FURTHER

In your worship time try to:

- Develop ideas for 'making all things new' by giving them new life.
- Raise an awareness of how much waste can be re-cycled.
- Develop a sense of responsibility for the regeneration of life in the local and wider environment.
- Explore what the implications of resurrection are in the way we treat our surroundings and fellow creatures.

Make a toy or model from junk. This could include egg boxes, yoghurt and margarine tubs, scraps of wool and material etc.

Arrange for someone from the local refuse disposal department to visit and talk about waste disposal and ways in which it may be recycled.

Make a list of all the organisations or centres in your community where rubbish can be taken for recycling.
Remember the less obvious collections of foil and used Christmas cards by various charitable organizations.

Watch the video *Care-takers* (includes the Re-Cycling Song — available on free loan from Christian Aid Marketing Resource, PO Box 100 London SE1 7RT)

Find a new use for a discarded item: e.g. Make a plant holder from a margarine tub, a pencil tidy from a washing up liquid bottle.

Find a discarded area of the school building or grounds and make plans to renew the area. Could a waste area be planted with seeds? Could a dull part of the corridor be brightened with art work or plants in pots?

SPRING TERM

USEFUL BOOKS

Re-Cycling for Change by Jon Vogler (published by Christian Aid).
Going Green at Home and School by John Howson (published by Wayland).

ON THE HOME STRAIGHT

Collective worship for the end of the week

GATHERING

Remind the children of the theme of seeing signs of resurrection. You may like to do this by showing some of the signs of new life the children have been creating.

LISTENING

Use this time to tell the story of Mother Theresa who brings resurrection to people others had left as worthless or dead.

MUSIC AND REFLECTION

Introduce the music and reflect on the opportunities we have each day to bring new life to something, or someone, near us.

HYMN

O Lord, all the world belongs to you *(Come and Praise No. 39)*

PRAYER

Lord of life and resurrection, Teach us to find new ways of living in which hope and courage overcome despair or sadness. May we be resurrection people bringing life and the possibility of new beginnings to all around us.

Amen

CLOSING REFRAIN

Shalom *(Come and Praise No. 141)*

THE SUMMER TERM

Introduction

The summer term tackles some more abstract ideas during worship time. It looks at why particular books, places, and people are special to certain groups. It begins to examine the significance of symbols in our lives and to explore the place of myths, dreams and imagination. Finally it looks at the experience of journeys and the meaning of pilgrimage. As the end of term approaches, and staff and pupils prepare to confront the changes which the passing of another school year will bring, it considers journeys of faith.

THEMES FOR THE SUMMER TERM

Theme 1 Something special

Week 1   Special books

Week 2   Special places

Week 3   Special people

Theme 2 Signs and symbols

Week 1   Thinking about signs and symbols

Week 2   The symbols of fire and wind

Week 3   The symbol of water

Theme 3 Myth, mystery and imagination

Week 1   True or false

Week 2   Myths and legends

Week 3   Dreams and visions

Theme 4 Journeys

Week 1   The experience of journeys

Week 2   Pilgrimages

Week 3   Journeys of faith

SUMMER TERM
THEME 1: *Something special*

Week 1
Special books

Week 2
Special places

Week 3
Special people

Checklist for Hymn Practice

The best gift *(Come and Praise No. 59)*
Who built the Ark *(Someone's singing Lord No. 44)*

The building song *(Come and Praise No. 61)*
By the waters of Babylon *(Alleluya, 77 songs for thinking people No. 68)*

Moses, I know you're the man *(Alleluya, 77 songs for thinking people No. 73)*
Joshua fit the battle of Jericho *(Alleluya, 77 songs for thinking people No. 70)*

■■■■ SUMMER TERM ■■■■

THEME 1: Week 1

THEME FOR THE WEEK
Special books

AIM: **To help the children understand that some things are special or holy and to find out about the sacred books of the religions of the world.**

 # SETTING OUT
Collective worship for the beginning of the week

 ## GATHERING
Introduce the idea of some things being special.

- Do the children have a special toy which they especially like?
- Do they have special stories which they like to hear again and again?
- Do they have a special book which means a lot to them? Is it kept in a special place and do they take special care of it.
- Explain that the story they will be listening to is about different things which were special to the family in the story.

 ## LISTENING

GRANNY'S BOX

The Baxtor family was busy. Mr and Mrs Baxtor, Sue and Andy were helping their Granny to move house. They had turned out the kitchen and the lounge and made a start on the garage. Today they had left Granny to sort out her bedroom whilst they looked at the loft. Mrs Baxtor had been up and down the ladder, passing things down to the waiting family below. There had been an old stair carpet, a broken chair, a box of storage jars and several other bits and pieces which Granny had stored away years ago. 'I think we've nearly finished,' yelled Mrs Baxtor from the loft doorway as she shone her torch around the loft for the last time. 'No, wait a minute, there's something here in the corner.' Sue and Andy craned their necks as they heard their mother pulling something across the boards above them.

'Be careful Mary,' called Mr Baxtor. 'Do you need a hand?'

SUMMER TERM

Mary Baxtor's grimy face appeared in the loft hatchway. 'It's a box,' she called, 'looks as if it's locked'.

At that moment Granny came out of her bedroom. 'Did you say you've found a box?' she enquired. 'That must be my special family box. I'd forgotten all about it'. Mary heaved the box to the loft entrance and Mr Baxtor balanced on the ladder and carefully eased it to the floor. It was wooden and covered in dust with a gold coloured lock on one side.

'It is my special box,' exclaimed Granny in delight. 'Oh we must stop for a cuppa and have a look'.

Mr Baxtor carried the box downstairs to the kitchen whilst Andy helped his Mum from the loft and Sue hurried to the kitchen and put the kettle on for coffee. Granny found a cloth and carefully dusted the box. She had no idea where the key was for the tiny key hole but Mr Baxtor managed to ease the lock open with a piece of wire. 'Oh this is exciting!' said Granny. 'There are all kinds of family treasures in here. Special things which I've kept for years.' The Baxtor family sat around the kitchen table and in turn took something from the box. 'Just look,' said Granny, 'this is a photograph of my mother's wedding'. The children pored over the photo whilst Granny explained who everyone was.

'Oh look here's a Valentine card you sent to Grandad. It's got the date in it and a little rhyme,' said Sue, as she turned the card over in her hands. 'Roses are red, violets are blue, sugar is sweet and I love you'. They all laughed.

'Not very poetic,' smiled Gran.

'This is interesting,' said Mr Baxtor. 'It's a newspaper cutting of the day the war ended. Look at the report of the celebrations in London.' He opened the piece of newspaper and a postcard fell to the floor.

Andy picked it up. 'It's from France and addressed to you Gran.'

Gran turned the card over and nodded as she read it out. 'Thank God for peace, see you soon darling, Maurice.'

'That was from Grandad when the war ended,' said Mrs Baxtor. 'What on earth is this?' she continued, as she unfolded a scrap of yellowing paper with beautiful copperplate handwriting on it.

Granny put on her glasses to look. 'Well fancy that, it's my mother's recipe for a cough linctus made out of lemon, glycerine and honey, and very good it was too,' she added. 'And bless her, look what she's written on the back. "Rules for life". '

Mrs Baxtor took the scrap of paper back and read aloud:
'Smile readily.
Forgive generously.
Pray daily.
Spread peace to all you meet.
Help when you can
and love always.'

'I wonder if she wrote that herself or if she copied it from a magazine or book? No way of knowing for sure, I suppose, but they look good rules to me anyway,' said Mr Baxtor.

The family spent a long time delving into Granny's special box discovering many treasures: photographs, letters, recipes, poems, articles from newspapers and magazines. All were things which had been saved because someone thought they were important. Important because they told of the family's history. Important because they

SUMMER TERM

reflected the values and hopes and ways of their family life. Important because the things in this box somehow linked them with the past and with the future.

'When I've settled into my new house, I shall buy a scrapbook and put all these things in it. It will be a book to tell us about our family.'

'Perhaps we can find some things to add to it and keep the record up to date,' said Andy.

'What a good idea,' said Granny. 'It will be a special book for us to read and enjoy together.'

 ## MUSIC AND REFLECTION

Introduce the music and ask the children to imagine that they are making a special family book. What would they put in it?

 ## HYMN

The best gift *(Come and Praise No. 59)*

 ## PRAYER

We thank God for all the things which we value and are special to us. Help us to understand why some things are of real worth.

Amen

 ## CLOSING REFRAIN

Shalom *(Come and Praise No. 141)*

TRAVELLING FURTHER

In your worship time try to:

- Identify what makes us regard some books as special (something which has belonged to the family for a long time, something given to us by a special person, something which reminds us of a person or event).
- Discuss whether special books are necessarily of monetary value.
- Develop the idea of groups of people having books which are special to the whole group; e.g. The Bible for Christians, The Torah for the Jews, The *Adi Granth* for Sikhs and The Koran for Muslims.

SUMMER TERM

Make a 'Special Book' for the class. Include favourite stories or poems, recipes or pictures. Discuss where to put the book in the class room and how it is to be treated.

Find out about the special book of Christians.

Find out about the special books of Jews, Muslims, or Sikhs.

Tell the children or ask them to find a favourite story from one of the religions special books.

USEFUL BOOKS

How the Bible came to us by Meryl Doney (published by Lion).
Holy Books by Jon Mayled (published by Wayland).

ON THE HOME STRAIGHT
Collective worship for the end of the week

GATHERING

Remind the children about the theme of special books.
Share what they have discovered about special books during the week.

LISTENING

Tell the story of Noah's ark which is common to both the Jewish and Christian traditions (Genesis 6. 9 – 8, 22). Use a version of the story from a children's Bible. Alternatively you may prefer to choose a story from another major religion.

USEFUL BOOKS

Buddhist Stories by J Snelling (published by Wayland).
Chinese Stories by Dr S Thompson (published by Wayland).
Hindu Stories by V P (Hement) Kanitkar (published by Wayland).

MUSIC AND REFLECTION

Introduce the music and ask the children to reflect on what they have discovered about special books during the week.

■ SUMMER TERM ■

 ## HYMN
Who built the Ark *(Someone's singing Lord No. 44)*

 ## PRAYER
We give thanks for all we can learn from special books about goodness and generosity and the love of our God.

Amen

 ## CLOSING REFRAIN
Shalom *(Come and Praise No. 141)*

THEME 1: Week 2

THEME FOR THE WEEK
Special places

AIM: To encourage the children to think about special places and to look at some buildings which have a special significance for world faiths.

SETTING OUT
Collective worship for the beginning of the week

GATHERING

Ask the children if they have ever made a secret den. What was special about it and what did they put in it?

LISTENING

A SPECIAL PLACE

The idea came to Bill at the beginning of the school summer holiday. He would make a den, a special place of his own. He looked around his garden. It was very small, more of a back yard really but his Mum grew a few flowers in the tiny flower bed and had even trained some sweet peas to twine up the fence. Where could he make a den? In the corner of the yard was a small shed where Bill kept his bike and his Mum kept her gardening tools. There was a narrow space between the back of the shed and the fence. Bill looked at the space and thought he could make a den there.

He worked all morning. First of all he wedged an old piece of wood between the back of the shed and the two fences to make a roof. Then he found an old sack which he hung from the roof to make a door. Now he was ready to organise the inside of the den. What would he need? Something to make the ground more comfortable, something to put possessions in and perhaps somewhere to put food. Bill went indoors, where his Mum was peeling potatoes at the sink, then into the hall to the cupboard under the stairs, where his Mum kept things she did not really need any more but did not want to throw away. He rummaged around. He found an old piece of left over carpet and an empty biscuit tin, with holly and ivy round the edge, which had been a present at Christmas. Bill dragged them out and took them to his mum. 'Do you mind if I have these?' He asked.

'What on earth for?' Mum queried. Bill did not answer. He wanted to keep his den a secret. Mother smiled, 'OK then, I don't suppose I've got any use for them really.'

Bill put the carpet down in his den and sat down. Things were beginning to take shape. What else could he do to make it feel special? Perhaps he would bring a few comics and a pack of cards. He could even ask for some biscuits and an apple for feasts there. He went into the kitchen to find the food. He could see his mum sitting down drinking a cup of tea. 'Can I help myself to some food?' Bill asked. 'Surely,' said Mum, 'just let me sit here for a while.' He took, an apple from the fruit bowl and two biscuits before returning to the den. This was going to be his special place, where he could come to read, play or just to think. He pulled the sacking across the front entrance and leant back. It felt good.

 ## MUSIC AND REFLECTION

Introduce the music and ask the children to imagine a special place they would like to make for themselves.

 ## HYMN

The building song *(Come and Praise No. 61)*

 ## PRAYER

We give thanks for special places where we can rest, think and relax. Help us to be aware of the needs of others to have space and peace too.

Amen

 ## CLOSING REFRAIN

Shalom *(Come and Praise No. 141)*

140

TRAVELLING FURTHER

In your worship time try to:

- Help the children to explore what kind of place makes them feel at ease and relaxed.
- Foster an understanding of what makes some buildings special for some people.
- Raise an awareness of the special buildings associated with major religious beliefs (church, temple, mosque, synagogue).
- Discover what religious buildings are used for.

In small groups discuss and then draw an ideal special place of their own.

With the children, plan a room or small area in the school which could be 'special'. How would it be decorated and furnished and what would it be used for?

Find out about a Christian church, a Jewish synagogue or a Hindu temple.

Arrange for a small group to visit a church or synagogue and report back to the class.

USEFUL BOOKS

Religious Buildings, Religious Topic Series (published by Wayland).
Exploring Religion - Buildings by Olivia Bennet (published by Bell and Hyman Ltd).
What to look for outside a church by P J Hunt (published by Ladybird).
What to look for inside a church by P J Hunt (published by Ladybird).
Places of Worship Exploring a Theme series (published by Christian Education Movement).

SUMMER TERM

ON THE HOME STRAIGHT
Collective worship for the end of the week

 GATHERING

Remind the children of the theme of special places.

 LISTENING

Arrange for a group of children to share what they have found out about churches, synagogues or mosques. Alternatively tell the story of the special temple that Solomon built in Jerusalem. Use a children's Bible or adapt the story to be found in 1 Kings 6.1 – 8.66.

 MUSIC AND REFLECTION

Introduce the music and ask the children to think about all the special talents needed to build a special place.

 HYMN

By the waters of Babylon *(Alleluya 77 songs for thinking people No. 68)*

Explain that this hymn is based on Psalm 137 and was sung when the Israelites were in exile in Babylon and could not visit their special place, the Temple in Jerusalem.

 PRAYER

In a moment of stillness let us think of all the special places in our (town, city, village, community). Let us give thanks for these special places and grow to understand and respect what they mean to those who use them.

Amen

CLOSING REFRAIN

Shalom *(Come and Praise No. 141)*

SUMMER TERM

THEME 1: Week 3

THEME FOR THE WEEK
Special people

AIM: **to explore what makes some people special and to find out about the special leaders of the main religions of the world.**

SETTING OUT
Collective worship for the beginning of the week

 GATHERING

Remind the children of the theme 'What is special' and introduce the theme of special people.

- Ask the children if there are some people they know but haven't met who are special for them (football heroes, pop stars, television personalities, historical personalities)?
- What do they admire about these people (skills, way of life, personality, achievements)?
- Do they try to imitate these people (by wearing similar clothes, behaving in the same way, using the same expressions).
- Explain that there are some special people who have been seen as very special for millions of people for hundreds and hundreds of years. They are people whose lives and teachings have become a model for other people.

 LISTENING

Introduce the following story which tells of the birth of the most famous leader of the Israelites who is a very special person for the Jewish people.

Long ago the Israelites lived in Egypt. The Israelites were slaves to the Egyptians. The King of the Egyptians, called the Pharaoh, was suspicious of the Israelites and said, 'There are so many Israelites and I fear that if a war was to break out the Israelites would join the enemy and fight against us. I will order that all Israelite boys who are born should be thrown into the river Nile and drowned.'

One of the Israelite women had a beautiful baby boy. She was determined that he should not be drowned so she managed to hide him for three months but then he became too big to hide. Then the Israelite mother had an idea. She took a rush basket and made it watertight with clay and tar. Then she put her baby boy into the basket and hid him amongst the reeds by the banks of the River Nile. The baby's sister, Miriam, hid nearby to keep watch. Now it happened that the Pharaoh's daughter came to bathe

---

in the river with her slaves. She noticed the basket amongst the reeds and sent one of her slaves to fetch it. When she looked in the basket she saw the baby and he was crying. 'It is a little Hebrew boy,' said the princess, sad to see the baby so upset.

Then Miriam, the baby's sister, came out of her hiding place and said, 'Shall I go and find a woman to look after the baby for you?'

'That would be a wonderful idea,' said the princess.

So Miriam ran as fast as she could to find her mother. 'Come quickly,' she panted, 'the princess has found our baby and wants someone to look after him.' Miriam's mother ran back immediately with her to the water's edge.

'Here is the baby,' said the princess, 'I want you to feed him and look after him until he is bigger. I will call him Moses because I pulled him out of the water.'

Moses grew up in the Egyptian Palace but he never forgot that he was an Israelite and when he was older he led his people out of Egypt to freedom in a new country.

MUSIC AND REFLECTION

Introduce the music and ask the children to reflect on the story of how the baby Moses was saved to be a special person for his people.

HYMN

Moses I know you're the man (Alleluya, 77 songs for thinking people No. 73)

PRAYER

We give thanks for special people to guide us and give us the example of courage, faith and hope.

Amen

CLOSING REFRAIN

Shalom (Come and Praise No. 141)

TRAVELLING FURTHER
In your worship time try to:

- Explore the qualities of leadership.
- Extend the children's knowledge of great leaders of world faiths.

Find out more about Moses. Using a children's version of the Bible tell the story of:

Moses and the burning bush.
Moses and the Exodus from Egypt.
Moses and the giving of the ten commandments.

In small groups, ask the children to collect together all they know about Jesus the leader of the Christian faith (where he was born, the name of his mother, where he lived, one of the stories he told, where and how he died, how he wanted others to live).

Find out about Siddhartha Gautama and the foundations of the Buddhist religion.

Find out about Muhammad and the faith of Islam.

Find out about Krishna and the Hindu faith.

USEFUL BOOKS

Founders of Religions by Tony D Triggs (published by Wayland).
Teachers and Prophets by Jon Mayled, Religious Topics Series, (published by Wayland).
Separate books on Buddhism, Christianity, Hinduism, Islam, Judaism, Sikhism from Religions of the World Series (published by Wayland).

ON THE HOME STRAIGHT
Collective worship for the end of the week

 GATHERING

Remind the children of the theme of special people who were leaders.

 LISTENING

Using a children's Bible tell the story of Joshua, a great leader of the Israelites, and the battle of Jericho (Joshua 6. 1 – 16, 20) or arrange for the children to act out or tell one of the stories they know about a special leader.

 MUSIC AND REFLECTION

Introduce the music and ask the children to focus on one leader they have found out about. What makes that leader special?

 HYMN

Joshua fit the battle of Jericho *(Alleluya, 77 songs for thinking people No. 70 and Junior Praise No. 143)* or use a hymn or song related to the story they have heard.

 PRAYER

We give thanks for the special people who have taught us how to live. May we try to follow their leadership and example.

Amen

 CLOSING REFRAIN

Shalom *(Come and Praise No. 141)*

146

SUMMER TERM
THEME 2: *Signs and symbols*

Week 1
Thinking about signs and symbols

Week 2
The symbols of fire and wind

Week 3
The symbol of water

Checklist for Hymn Practice

The bell of creation *(Come and Praise No. 86)*
From the darkness came light *(Come and Praise No. 29)*

Light up the fire *(Come and Praise No. 55)*
Spirit of God *(Come and Praise No. 63)*

Desert Rain *(Come and Praise No. 77)*
Water of Life *(Come and Praise No. 2)*

◼ SUMMER TERM ◼

THEME 2: Week 1

THEME FOR THE WEEK
Thinking about signs and symbols

AIM: **To raise an awareness of the signs and symbols which we use in everyday life and to look at some religious symbols.**

SETTING OUT
Collective worship for the beginning of the week (This will need preparation beforehand.)

✕↓✕ GATHERING

Prepare a collection of signs and symbols; e.g. a large picture of a road sign, the scarf of a football team, a national flag, a cross, a badge of a well known organization, a wedding ring.

● Identify each item and discuss its significance with the children. (The road sign gives an instruction or warning. Wearing a particular football scarf signifies support for the club. A Union Jack represents the British Isles. A cross is a symbol of the Christian faith. A ring can be a symbol of a special relationship between two people.)
● Encourage the children to think of other signs and symbols they use (shop signs, road signs, badges, flags, uniforms etc).

 LISTENING

Ask the children to listen to the following story and to see how many signs and symbols they can notice.

A WALK TO SCHOOL

Jim and Sally were walking to school. They passed several shops: the bakers with its smell of freshly baked bread, the barbers with **the red and white pole** outside and a pub called the Three Bells. **The board with the three golden bells** painted on it swung in the wind as they walked by. At the end of the road they crossed by the zebra crossing. 'Wait for **the green man**,' warned Jim. Safely across, they saw Martin and Kirsty walking ahead of them. 'Look Martin is wearing his **Spurs football scarf**,' said Jim, 'his Dad bought it for his birthday. He's a really keen Spurs supporter.'

They hurried along to catch up with their friends. Walking on through the town they passed the town hall. 'Why is **the Union Jack** flying?' asked Kirsty.

Summer Term

'I suppose it's a special day. Is it the Queen's birthday or something?' Sally replied.

'I don't know,' said Jim, 'but Sal have you got any money? I fancy dropping into the corner shop to buy some crisps.'

Sally felt in her pocket. 'No luck I'm afraid, but look what I have found.' She pulled out her **handkerchief with a knot tied in the corner**. 'I tied the knot to remind me of something. What was it? Yes I've remembered, it's my turn to feed the class hamster. Come on you three or I'll be too late.'

The friends quickened their pace but just as they reached the street where their school was they saw a policeman standing in the middle of the road. He was **holding up his hand** to stop the traffic. Some workmen were just starting to repair the road and the policeman was directing the traffic in a single file. The children walked by the workmen's hut and hurried into the playground just in time to hear **the bell ring** to signal the time to go in.

MUSIC AND REFLECTION

Introduce the music and ask the children to think of their own journey to school. What signs or symbols did they pass?

HYMN

The bell of creation *(Come and Praise No. 86)*
In this hymn the bell is used as a symbol of the creation and of the life in us.

PRAYER

Let us open our eyes to see the symbols and signs around us which speak of God's love.

Amen

CLOSING REFRAIN

Shalom *(Come and Praise No. 141)*

▄▄▄▄▄▄ Sᴜᴍᴍᴇʀ Tᴇʀᴍ ▄▄▄

TRAVELLING FURTHER
In your worship time try to:

● Help the children to be aware of the variety of signs around them.
● Develop an understanding of the meaning of symbols.

Make a class exhibition of symbols and signs. Take time to discuss the meaning of each sign and symbol.

Discuss the symbols and signs found in the story 'A walk to school'.

Design a sign for a shop (bakers, opticians, craft shop).

Find out about some of the signs and symbols used by Christianity, Judaism, Hinduism or Islam. A collage could be made of the symbols.

Some examples of Christian symbols are:

A Cross – a reminder of Jesus' death on the cross and a symbol of his love for us.
Candles – a reminder of Jesus as the light of the world.
A shepherd's crook – a symbol of Jesus as the good shepherd.
A Dove – a symbol of the Holy Spirit or peace.
A Rainbow – a symbol of God's promise never to flood the world again.
A fish – a symbol of Jesus and his followers.

USEFUL BOOKS

Religious Symbols by Jon Mayled (published by Wayland).
Signs and Symbols by Olivia Bennett, Exploring Religion series (published by Bell and Hyman).
'Signs and Symbols' series (published by Wayland).

━━━━━━━━━━ **SUMMER TERM** ━━━━━━━━━━

ON THE HOME STRAIGHT
Collective worship for the end of the week

 GATHERING

Remind the children of the theme of signs and symbols.

 LISTENING

Arrange for the children to present the symbols which they have collected or drawn and to speak about them; e.g. this is a picture of the Jewish flag. It is a symbol of Judaism. It has on it the star of David with six points. Long ago David was a famous King and some people think that the star is like the shield used by King David.

 MUSIC AND REFLECTION

Introduce the music and use one of the symbols as a focus for reflection; e.g. light a candle and say: Let us look at this candle and think of what the symbol of its light means to you.

 HYMN

From the darkness came light *(Come and Praise No. 29) (or choose another song suitable for the symbol on which you have focussed.)*

 PRAYER

Use a prayer related to the focus of the reflection or use the following if the symbol of light has been used.

As we look at this light we give thanks for all it symbolizes for us as we remember that lights can guide us and comfort us in the darkness.

Amen

 CLOSING REFRAIN

Shalom *(Come and Praise No. 141)*

SUMMER TERM

THEME 2: Week 2

THEME FOR THE WEEK
The symbols of fire and wind

AIM: **To explore the symbols of wind and fire.**

SETTING OUT
Collective worship for the beginning of the week

 GATHERING

Remind the children of the theme of signs and symbols.

- **What is a symbol?**
  A symbol is a mark or artefact which recalls or represents an idea or association of ideas; e.g. a wedding ring reminds us of the commitment of two people to each other and of continual love.
- **What is a sign?**
  A sign is a mark or gesture which gives information; e.g. a circle to indicate a roundabout.

- What signs or symbols did the children discover last week?
- Can they recognize any signs or symbols around them now? (For example school badge emblems, flags, crosses, wedding rings etc.)

 LISTENING

Explain that during the week the focus will be on two special symbols. Listen to the following riddles to guess what the symbols are.

- **Riddle 1**
  You cannot see me but you can see what I do. Sometimes you can hear me and my voice can be very gentle. When I am strong my voice can scream and moan. I can lift a feather so gently you won't know I am there but I can also knock down the tallest tree or crash the biggest ship at sea. What am I?

- **Riddle 2**
  My colours can be red or yellow or sometimes green or blue. I crackle and hiss and can leap and spark. When I am controlled I can be useful and give both warmth and light but don't play with me for I am powerful and can destroy. What am I?

SUMMER TERM

MUSIC AND REFLECTION

Introduce the music and ask the children to reflect on wind or fire. What do they like or dislike about them?

HYMN

Light up the fire *(Come and Praise No. 55)*

PRAYER

We give thanks for the warmth and light of fire. May they remind us of God's care and strength. May we be warmed by love and led by the spirit of peace.

Amen

CLOSING REFRAIN

Shalom *(Come and Praise No. 141)*

TRAVELLING FURTHER

In your worship time try to:

- Help the children to explore as many ideas about the symbols of fire and wind as possible.
- Use music, picture or story to foster associations of ideas about fire and wind.

Make a collage to show both the power and uses of either wind or fire. Show how both can be helpful or destructive (useful wind for windmills, sailing ships, flying kites; harmful wind blowing away the surface soil, causing damage by hurricanes or tornadoes. Fire for warmth, cooking, smelting; fire which destroys – forests or buildings).

Tell the story of Moses and the burning bush (Exodus 3. 1 – 11). Reflect on how fire can change substances to produce warmth, heat and light. Do the children know how Moses was changed after the experience of the burning bush? Are there ways in which God is like a fire?

Using a children's version of the Bible tell the story of Pentecost (Acts 2. 1 – 18). Discuss the symbols used to represent the Holy Spirit. How did the Holy Spirit affect the disciples?

Using a variety of materials make a flame picture. Around the picture write ideas about fire: fire can warm us when we feel cold and miserable; fire can give light in the dark; fire can burn things which we no longer need; fire can melt and change things; fire can kill germs; fire can sparkle and leap with life; fire is powerful.

■ SUMMER TERM ■

ON THE HOME STRAIGHT

Collective worship for the end of the week

 ## GATHERING

Remind the children of the theme of fire and wind and share some of the ideas they have explored during the week.

 ## LISTENING

Using a children's Bible tell the story of Pentecost (Acts 2. 1 – 18), explaining that fire and wind are both used as symbols of the Holy Spirit, or arrange for the children to present some of their work on fire or wind.

 ## MUSIC AND REFLECTION

Introduce the music and ask the children to reflect on the power and warmth of fire, the gentleness and strength of the wind and to think what they tell us about God's Holy Spirit?

 ## HYMN

Spirit of God *(Come and Praise No. 63)*

PRAYER

May the fire of God's love warm and encourage us.
May the sparkle of God's love give us light.
May the power of God's Holy Spirit strengthen us.

Amen

CLOSING REFRAIN

Shalom *(Come and Praise No. 141)*

SUMMER TERM

THEME 2: Week 3

THEME FOR THE WEEK
The symbol of water

AIM: **To explore the idea of water as a symbol**

SETTING OUT
Collective worship for the beginning of the week (This will need preparation beforehand.)

 GATHERING

Remind the children of the theme of symbols. What is a symbol? Which symbols did we explore last week? Explain that this week we will be thinking about another symbol.

 LISTENING

You will need: A large jug of water which is hidden out of sight. On to a table place a bottle of squash which needs diluting, a mug, a vase, a few flowers and a small wash bowl with soap and towel.

Ask three volunteers to:
● Make a drink of squash.
● Arrange the flowers in a vase.
● Wash their hands.

Can they do these tasks satisfactorily?
What do they all need?

● Supply the jug of water so that the tasks can be completed.

What do we need water for? (sustaining our life and the lives of plants and animals, washing and cleaning jobs, recreation)

Can water be thought of as a symbol?
What might water symbolize? (life, cleanliness, power)

SUMMER TERM

 MUSIC AND REFLECTION

Introduce the music and ask the children to reflect on the importance of water in their lives.

 HYMN

Desert rain *(Come and Praise No. 77)*

 PRAYER

We give thanks for the gift of water.
For water to drink and quench our thirst.
For water to wash away dirt and grime.
For water to sustain plants and trees and all living things.
For water for swimming, sailing and playing.

Amen

 CLOSING REFRAIN

Shalom *(Come and Praise No. 141)*

TRAVELLING FURTHER

In your worship time try to:

- Explore the importance of water to sustain life.
- Explore how water can be a symbol of life and the washing away of sin.
- Introduce the idea of water as a symbol of God's life giving words.

Plant two trays of mustard and cress seeds. Water one of the trays of seeds regularly and leave the other tray dry. Let the children observe what happens.

Using a children's Bible look at the story of Jesus and the Samaritan woman (John 4. 1 – 30). In what ways is Jesus the 'living water'?

Give each child a piece of paper in the shape of a raindrop. Ask them to draw a picture to show just one use of water. (For example cooking vegetables, making a drink, washing clothes, yachting, fishing, watering the garden etc.) Mount the pictures under the heading 'The Water of life'.

Find out about the act of baptism in the Christian faith or the importance of the River Ganges to the Hindus. If possible invite a priest to talk about baptism or visit a church to look at a font.

■ SUMMER TERM ■

ON THE HOME STRAIGHT
Collective worship for the end of the week

 GATHERING

Remind the children of the theme of symbols and of the focus on water this week.

 LISTENING

Ask the children to listen carefully to the following passage and to make pictures in their mind about it.

God visits the earth with the waters of heaven providing it with rain, softening it with showers and blessing its growth.
The Lord makes springs to break out and rivers to run between the hills.
The wild beasts quench their thirst and the birds of the air rest on the river banks.
The Lord will satisfy our needs in the heat so that we will be like a well watered garden, like a spring whose waters never fail.

As a deer longs for running streams so do I long for your words O God.
Come to God all who are thirsty.
Come and listen to the words of God and you shall have life.
As the rain and snow come down from heaven making the earth blossom and bear fruit,
So shall God's words give life.

Jesus said, 'The water that I shall give will be like an inner spring always welling up for eternal life. Whoever drinks the water I shall give will never thirst again.'

(Adapted from the Psalms, Isaiah and John's Gospel).

 MUSIC AND REFLECTION

Introduce the music and ask the children to reflect on one of the pictures they enjoyed from the reading.

 HYMN

Water of life *(Come and Praise No. 2)*

 PRAYER

God who blesses us with rain and showers and brings life to the dry earth, help us to listen to your words and be refreshed by your water of life.

Amen

 CLOSING REFRAIN

Shalom *(Come and Praise No. 141)*

SUMMER TERM
THEME 3: *Myth, mystery and imagination*

Week 1
True or false

Week 2
Myths and legends

Week 3
Dreams and visions

Checklist for Hymn Practice

Happiness is *(Alleluya, 77 songs for thinking people No. 5)*
A still small voice *(Come and Praise No. 96)*

Who put the colours in the rainbow *(Come and Praise No. 12)*
Somebody greater *(Come and Praise No. 5)*

If I had a hammer *(Come and Praise No. 71)*
Last night I had the strangest dream *(Alleluya, 77 songs for thinking people No. 45)*
Peace is flowing like a river *(Come and Praise No. 144)*

═══════════ SUMMER TERM ═══════════

THEME 3: Week 1

THEME FOR THE WEEK
True or false

AIM: To help the children appreciate the varieties of ways the same events can be interpreted and to understood and reflect on what is meant by 'true'.

SETTING OUT
Collective worship for the beginning of the week

 GATHERING

Ask the children to listen carefully to the following sentences and questions and to answer them as truthfully as possible. Discuss one group at a time.

- Buckingham Palace is in London.
- The leaves of the Holly tree are prickly.
- When water freezes it becomes ice.

- Is the sky blue?
- Is the sky orange?

Are these sentences more accurate:
- The sky is sometimes blue.
- The sky is sometimes orange.

Which of these sentences is true?
- An elephant is big.
- A mouse is big.

What would make them more accurate?
- Compared to a mouse an elephant is big.
- Compared to a flea a mouse is big.

Summer Term

LISTENING

Explain that the following two readings are accounts of the same football match.

This account is by Mr Barton, a regular supporter of Wimbury Town Football Club.

Wimbury Town's performance last Saturday in the match against their old rivals Matcham United was a great disappointment. Harris scored an amazing goal from a skilful pass by Moody to put Wimbury in the lead in the first three minutes of the game. Throughout the first half Wimbury was in possession of the ball for most of the time. But despite valiant work by Grandfield, who carved up United's defence, Wimbury seemed unable to score. Just before half time a careless cross by Wimbury's mid field player, Geoff Soames, allowed United to equalize.

During the second half United was on top form with two more goals in the net within ten minutes. The first followed an amazing run by the United captain, Swells, and the second headed into the net by Owen. With the score at 3-1 to United, nothing seemed to be going right for Wimbury. Their defence was so ragged and disorganized that Clarke misjudged a pass and scored an own goal, allowing United to romp home with a 4-1 win.

The second account of the same match is by Bobby, Mr Barton's son, who was going to a football match with his Dad for the first time.

There were loads of people hurrying along the streets to the ground. When we got there we had to queue up and go through a turnstile where Dad paid the money for our tickets. I was wearing my new football scarf. Dad carried a box for me to stand on, so that I could see better. There were so many people but on my box I could see pretty well. There was a huge cheer when the players came out. Our team players were wearing red and white and the other team were in blue shirts and shorts. The crowd sang songs to cheer on their teams. I couldn't hear all the words but I joined in as best I could. When half time came Dad and I ate the cake which mum had packed up for us. Dad poured us a hot cup of tea from the Thermos flask. I was glad to warm my hands on the mug as I had forgotten my gloves and my hands were freezing. When we got home I looked through the programme Dad had bought. It was a smashing match but we didn't win.

MUSIC AND REFLECTION

Introduce the music and ask the children to think about the two accounts of the match. How were they different? Were they both true?

Were Mr Barton and Bobby happy with their afternoon out?

HYMN

Happiness is (*Alleluya, 77 songs for thinking people No. 5*)

SUMMER TERM

PRAYER

May we always try to seek the truth. May we always try to speak the truth. May we always be ready to listen to others and try to understand what they see as the truth.

Amen

CLOSING REFRAIN

Shalom *(Come and Praise No. 141)*

TRAVELLING FURTHER

In your worship time try to:

- Give opportunities to compare experiences or accounts of experiences.
- Raise an awareness of different outlooks and opinions.
- Foster a respect for different points of view.
- Develop an awareness of how previous experiences of life can influence how we interpret events.

Look more closely at the two stories of the football match. What kind of information does Mr Barton's account give? How is Bobby's account different? Why do you think they are different? Are they both true?

Working in pairs ask the children to draw one of the following: play time at our school, the head teacher, listening to a story. Compare their results. What is similar? What is different?

Working in pairs give each pair a copy of the accounts of 'The great feast', a story Jesus told, found in Matthew 22. 1 – 14 and Luke 14. 16 – 24. How do they differ? Which parts are the same? Do you think they are based on the same story? Could they both be true?

This will need preparation beforehand.

Choose one child to perform a simple action; e.g. make a cheese and cucumber sandwich. Ask another child to record in note form **exactly** what happens as it is happening. Later, ask two other children to describe what happened and compare it with the recorder's version. Do they remember the same points? Do they remember accurately? How do their accounts differ?

■ SUMMER TERM ■

ON THE HOME STRAIGHT
Collective worship for the end of the week

 ## GATHERING
Remind the children of the theme of discovering what is meant by true or false.

 ## LISTENING
Read the following story to the children.

JESUS UNDERSTANDS THE TRUTH OF WHAT HE SEES

One day Jesus was standing at the entrance of the Temple. He was watching people putting their gifts of money into the big chest of the Temple treasury. Many rich and important people dropped in their large gifts. Then Jesus saw a poor woman approach. She was a widow and had very little money. She put two tiny coins into the chest.

Ask the children who they think gave the most. Then complete the reading of the story.

Jesus said 'The poor widow has given more than any of them. For the rich, who have given, have more than enough but the widow woman, who had so little, gave all that she had to live on.'

 ## MUSIC AND REFLECTION
Introduce the music and ask the children to think about how Jesus understood the truth of what he saw.

 ## HYMN
A still small voice *(Come and Praise No. 96)*

 ## PRAYER
May we look at all around us, with love and compassion.
May we listen, with care and understanding.
May we speak, with truth and insight.

Amen

 ## CLOSING REFRAIN
Shalom *(Come and Praise No. 141)*

━━━━━━━━━ **SUMMER TERM** ━━━━━━━━━

THEME 3: Week 2

THEME FOR THE WEEK
Myths and legends

AIM: **To help the children understand what is meant by a myth and to familiarize them with some of the myths of various traditions.**

SETTING OUT
Collective worship for the beginning of the week

GATHERING

Tell the children that there are some very ancient stories throughout the world which ancestors told to help explain traditions and the world's mysteries. These stories are called 'myths' or sometimes 'legends'. The myths helped people to understand something about the world and the way people behaved; e.g. how the world was created, where plants and animals originate. Explain that these stories were written or told long ago before there was much scientific knowledge.

LISTENING

The following myth is based on a story from China which tells about the beginning of the world.

Long long ago before the beginning of time there was nothing but chaos and emptiness and all was dark and covered in mist. Then a great colourful light pierced the mist and all which was light floated upwards and formed the heaven whilst all that was heavy sank and formed the earth.

Two great and powerful forces emerged. One was like a fierce and fiery dragon and was called Yang. The other was in the form of a misty cloud and was called Yin. The fiery dragon produced the sun, whilst moist and misty Yin created the silvery moon. Together Yin and Yang developed the four seasons and the elements of water, fire, earth, metal and wood. Then together Yin and Yang made a giant called P'an Ku. Now P'an Ku grew bigger every year of his life and every year he worked shaping the earth. He dug out river valleys and heaped the earth and rocks to form mountains. But at last the day came when the mighty P'an Ku, exhausted by his work, collapsed and died. So great was his body that when it fell to the ground it formed the five holy mountains of China. Great rivers and oceans were formed from his blood and his bones became rocks. Plants and trees, living creatures and men and women all came from the body of the great P'an Ku.

THEME 3: Week 2

SUMMER TERM

MUSIC AND REFLECTION

Introduce the music and ask the children to reflect on how they think the world began.

HYMN

Who put the colours in the rainbow? *(Come and Praise No. 12)*

PRAYER

We give thanks for the wonder of Creation and for all stories which help us to understand the world around us.

Amen

CLOSING REFRAIN

Shalom *(Come and Praise No. 141)*

TRAVELLING FURTHER

In your worship time try to:

- Introduce the children to myths from different traditions.
- Help the children to comprehend that great myths contain truths which help us to understand the world around us.

Invite the children to write or tell a story to explain something about the world around them; e.g. why the sea is salt. How the stars were put in the sky. Why people speak different languages.

Tell the children one of the Creation stories.

Ask the children to write or tell a story which explains something about a creature they like; e.g. how the elephant got its trunk, why cats have whiskers, how the zebra got its stripes.

Make a frieze depicting the creation story found in Genesis 1. 1 – 2, 4.

SUMMER TERM

USEFUL BOOKS

Gods and men, Myths and legends from the world's religions by J Bailey, K Mcleish and D Spearman (published by Oxford University Press).
Worlds of Difference by Martin Palmer and Esther Bisset (published by Blackie).
Creation Stories by Jon Mayled (published by Wayland).

ON THE HOME STRAIGHT
Collective worship for the end of the week

GATHERING

Remind the children about the theme of myths and ask them to tell you what they understand by 'myth'. Tell them that what you are going to read is found in the special book of both the Jewish faith and the Christian faith. Explain that very many people believe this is exactly the way the world was created. Others consider it a very important and beautiful story which tells about the purpose of creation and about the way God sees creation and the place of men and women. Ask the children to listen for the words, 'God saw that it was good,' which are repeated after nearly all of God's creative acts.

LISTENING

Read from the New English Bible the creation story from Genesis 1. 1 – 2, 4.

MUSIC AND REFLECTION

Introduce the music and ask the children to reflect on the wonder of all that is on the earth and how the story tells us that God loved all that He had made.

HYMN

Somebody greater *(Come and Praise No. 5)*

PRAYER

We think with awe and wonder of the creation of the world and all that is in it. We give thanks for the sun, moon and stars, and for all the amazing varieties of trees plants and animals. For earth and sky, fire and water, we give praise and thanks.

Amen

CLOSING REFRAIN

Shalom *(Come and Praise No. 141)*

THEME 3: Week 3

THEME FOR THE WEEK
Dreams and visions

AIM: to reflect on how dreams can inspire us and to famialiarize the children with some famous dreams and visions.

SETTING OUT
Collective worship for the beginning of the week

 ## GATHERING

Remind the children of the main theme of 'Myth, mystery and imagination' and introduce this week's theme of 'Dreams and visions'. Ask them what they understand by the word dream.

- Is it something you imagine happening when asleep? For example a dream of your cat suddenly being able to talk.
- Is it something you hope might happen? For example day-dreaming whilst still awake of scoring the winning goal for your team.

Ask the children what they understand by the word vision.

- Is it something seen in the imagination? For example a vision of angels.
- Is it an idea of something special. For example a vision of a perfect world without war or fighting.

Introduce the story: The man with a dream.

LISTENING

It was August 28th 1963. The wide avenue which leads to the Lincoln Memorial in Washington D.C. was packed with people. People of all ages and ethnic backgrounds, alongside each other waving placards and signs, applauding and cheering. They had come from all over the United States of America. In front of the crowd, beneath the shadow of the statue of Abraham Lincoln, under the blaze of lights and television cameras, stood a group of people including the folk singers Bob Dylan and Joan Baez and the group Peter Paul and Mary.

SUMMER TERM

As Joan Baez sang the last notes of the song, 'We shall overcome', someone stepped forward to the microphone. A great cheer went up from all the crowd to greet the man. His name was Martin Luther King.

Martin Luther King was black. For most of his adult life he had campaigned for the rights of the black people of America. He wanted all people to enjoy the same freedom and opportunities. He wanted them to be able to shop in the same shops as white people, go to the same schools, cinemas and restaurants, be assured of the same rights. Many of the white people in America supported his campaign and the President of the United States, John F. Kennedy had approved of this march to Washington. However, not everyone agreed with the President or with Martin Luther King. Many people tried to frighten Martin Luther King. They sent him threatening letters and his house was bombed. On several occasions he was imprisoned and on one visit to New York he was stabbed and seriously wounded. Martin Luther King often went in fear of his life but, despite all the violence he and other black people experienced, he never used violence himself. At all times he encouraged his supporters to use only peaceful ways to bring about the justice and freedom they wanted.

Now as he began to speak the vast crowd of thousands of people were silent listening to his every word. He spoke of his hopes and dreams for the future. He spoke of his dreams of all people, black and white, being treated as equal. He spoke of his dream of when all the people of the world whatever their colour, race or religion would live together in peace and harmony.

As he spoke the thousands of people listening to him were caught up with his dreams of justice and peace. They wanted to help him make his dream come true.

MUSIC AND REFLECTION

Introduce the music and ask the children to reflect on Martin Luther King's dream. Has part of his dream come true?

HYMN

Last night I had the strangest dream (*Alleluya, 77 songs for thinking people* No. 45)

PRAYER

We pray that we may listen to the dreams of others and be inspired by their visions.

Amen

CLOSING REFRAIN

Shalom (*Come and Praise No. 141*)

▬▬▬ Summer Term ▬▬

TRAVELLING FURTHER

In your worship time try to:

- Give opportunities to reflect on how dreams and visions can inspire us.
- Encourage reflection on how being a 'dreamer' may lead to amazing results.

Find out more about the life of Martin Luther King.

Tell the story of Joan of Arc.

Discuss or write a class description entitled 'My dream for . . . my life? our school? our town? our world?'

Tell and illustrate one of the following Bible stories. You may prefer to use a children's version of the story.

Jacob's dream (Genesis 28. 11 – 22).
Joseph's dream (Genesis 37. 2 – 11).
The wine steward and the baker tell Joseph their dreams (Genesis 39. 19 – 40. 23).
Pharoah's dream (Genesis 41. 1 – 57).

Learn the songs 'Any dream will do', or 'Pharoah's dreams explained', available in *Joseph and the Amazing Technicolour Dreamcoat* Lyrics by Tim Rice and music by Andrew Lloyd-Webber. Abridged Edition (published by Novello. ISBN 200122)

USEFUL BOOKS

Martin Luther King by Nigel Hunter, Great Lives Series (published by Wayland). ISBN 0 85078 563 4
Martin Luther King, by Nigel Richardson, Profiles Series (published by Hamish Hamilton). ISBN 0 241 10931 0

ON THE HOME STRAIGHT
Collective worship for the end of the week

 GATHERING

Remind the children of the theme of Dreams and visions and briefly talk about the variety of dreams they have been thinking about.

 LISTENING

Arrange for one of the children to present some of their work or read the following prayer of St Francis, a vision of how his life could be lived to bring peace.

Lord, make me an instrument of your peace,
Where there is hatred,let me sow love;
Where there is injury, pardon;
Where there is discord, union;
Where there is doubt, faith;
Where there is despair, hope;
Where there is darkness, light;
Where there is sadness, joy.

 MUSIC AND REFLECTION

Introduce the music and ask the children to reflect on a dream or vision of what they would alter if they could rule the world.

 HYMN

Peace is flowing like a river *(Come and Praise No. 144)*

 CLOSING REFRAIN

Shalom *(Come and Praise No. 141)*

SUMMER TERM
THEME 4: *Journeys*

Week 1
The experience of journeys

Week 2
Pilgrimages

Week 3
Journeys of faith

Checklist for Hymn Practice

The journey of life *(Come and Praise No. 45)*
Travel on *(Come and Praise No. 42)*

He who would valiant be *(Come and Praise No. 44)*
How lovely on the mountains *(Junior Praise No. 84)*

Father, hear the prayer we offer *(Come and Praise No. 48)*
You shall go out with joy *(Come and Praise No. 98)*

■■■■■■■ **SUMMER TERM** ■■■■■■■

THEME 4: Week 1

THEME FOR THE WEEK
The experience of journeys

AIM: **To help the children explore the experiences associated with journeys.**

SETTING OUT
Collective worship for the beginning of the week

 GATHERING

Introduce the idea of travelling and ask the children the following questions:

● Who will be going on a journey during the summer holidays?
● What is the most exciting journey they have had?
● What do they like about travelling?
● Are there things they dislike about travelling?

 LISTENING

Introduce and read the following story:

JASON'S JOURNEY

The bell for the end of school rang. Everyone packed away their books and began to put on their coats and collect their bags.

'You ready Jason?' asked his friend Michael.

'Have you forgotten? I'm staying with my Gran tonight as Mum and Dad are going out,' Jason replied.

'Where does she live?'

'I've got to catch a bus and then walk to my Gran's house.' Jason picked up his bag. It was heavy with the things he had packed this morning: pyjamas, toothbrush, towel and some favourite books and games. He had been to stay with his Gran loads of times but this was the first time he had travelled alone and he felt a bit nervous. He waved goodbye to Michael and hurried along to the bus stop. A bus was just coming along. Jason shaded his eyes to look at the number. No it wasn't the one he needed. He needed a 77. He stood in the queue. Two more buses came but not a 77. Jason shifted from one foot to the other. He hoped he was standing at the right bus stop. Just as he was wondering what to do a 77 bus arrived. 'Does this go to the Odeon cinema?' he asked the driver.

■ SUMMER TERM ■

'Indeed we do,' said the driver taking Jason's fare. Jason sat down at the front of the bus so he could see easily. How he was on his way he felt more confident. He looked out of the window at the street market and shops as the bus went along. Suddenly he saw the Odeon cinema flash by. He leapt up.

'I've missed my stop,' he yelled to the driver.

'Now just you wait,' said the driver. 'You can't get off while the bus is moving. I'll stop at the next stop just along here and you can walk back.'

Jason got off as soon as the bus stopped. He felt in his pocket for the map his Dad had drawn for him the night before. He read the instructions: 'Get off at the Odeon cinema and walk on to Endless Street. Turn left and follow the road. Belle View Road is on the left. Gran's house is number 66.' Once he had got his bearings it was easy. As he walked along Belle View Road he could see his Gran waiting at the window. She opened the door.

'Had a good journey dear?' she asked.

'No problems,' said Jason, feeling proud of himself.

 ## MUSIC AND REFLECTION

Introduce the music and ask the children to reflect on Jason's journey. Did he find it enjoyable? Were there any parts which were hard?

 ## HYMN

The journey of life *(Come and Praise No. 45)*

 ## PRAYER

May the road rise to meet you.
May the wind be always at your back.
May the sun shine warm upon your face,
The rains fall soft upon your fields and until we meet again
May God hold you in the palm of his hand.

A Celtic blessing

 ## CLOSING REFRAIN

Shalom *(Come and Praise No. 141)*

172

TRAVELLING FURTHER

In your worship time try to:

- Explore the good and bad experiences of journeys.
- Talk about the things that would help the children to feel confident about making a journey.
- Share strategies for making successful journeys.

Tell or act out the legend of St Christopher, the patron saint of travellers. (*Encyclopaedia Brittanica* includes information about St Christopher.)

Write a prayer or blessing to say before setting out on a journey.

Discuss the different preparations we need to make for various kinds of journeys; e.g. a day visit to the sea, a walk in the mountains, a weeks holiday abroad, a visit to a museum.

Share what makes travelling exciting and what makes it difficult. Make a class book of pictures and writing entitled 'The joys and pains of travel'.

Discuss or write about 'My most exciting journey'.

ON THE HOME STRAIGHT

Collective worship for the end of the week

GATHERING

Remind the children of the theme of Journeys.

LISTENING

Arrange for the children to tell or act out the story of St Christopher or share stories of their own journeys.

MUSIC AND REFLECTION

Introduce the music and ask the children to think of all those who are making journeys today.

SUMMER TERM

 ### HYMN
Travel On *(Come and Praise No. 42)*

 ### PRAYER
Use one of the blessings written by the children during the week.

 ### CLOSING REFRAIN
Shalom *(Come and Praise No. 141)*

THEME 4: Week 2

THEME FOR THE WEEK
Pilgrimages

AIM: to help the children understand the meaning of pilgrimage.

 SETTING OUT
Collective worship for the beginning of the week

 ### GATHERING
Remind the children that they have been thinking about journeys. Ask them if there is a place they would especially like to visit.

Tell the children that there are some places in the world which are visited by many people because they are thought to be holy. Do they know any? (e.g. Canterbury Cathedral, Glastonbury, St Peter's Basilica in Rome, Lourdes in France. Benares in India, Mecca in Saudi Arabia, Bethlehem and Jerusalem in the Holy Land.) Explain that people visit these places sometimes to thank their God for a blessing they have received, or to say sorry, or to ask for God's help. Tell the children that the people who make these special journeys are called pilgrims and that the journeys are called pilgrimages.

 ### LISTENING
Introduce the story about a pilgrimage Jesus made when he was about twelve.

A PILGRIMAGE TO JERUSALEM
Dawn was just breaking, but already everyone in Nazareth was awake and busy at work. The festival of the Passover was approaching and many villagers were preparing to travel to Jerusalem to celebrate the festival there. It would take them many days to walk to the city and they would have to camp out under the stars at night. Everyone, young and old, was helping to pack food, tents, blankets and pots for cooking. Jesus was getting ready with Joseph and Mary his mother. The travellers would set out together in a group. 'It's safer to travel together. Part of the road is isolated and there could be robbers about,' explained Joseph as he led their donkey from the stable. 'Ask Mary if the blankets are ready will you Jesus?' Jesus ran into the house, fetched the blankets from his mother and carried them back to Joseph, who strapped them onto the donkeys back. 'We'll need these at night-time,' said Joseph. 'It can be very cold sleeping out on the hillside. We'll have to make a fire to warm ourselves and cook the food.'

SUMMER TERM

The sun was still quite low in the sky as the villagers set out. Those who were too old or frail to make the journey stood at their doors to wave their friends and relatives off. Jesus skipped and ran alongside the donkey. There was an air of expectancy and excitement. The travellers soon separated out, the men walking with their staves at the front, the women strolling along chatting and the children racing in and out of the crowd.

By midday the sun was high in the sky and everyone was ready to rest. The leaders had led them to a well, where they could drink and refill their water skins. The company of travellers rested in the shade of rocks and trees until the heat of the day was past. Then, as the temperature dropped, they set out again. At night fall the travellers stopped to eat and to camp. They gathered wood to make a fire and sat huddled in their blankets exchanging news and stories. Some of the children had not been to Jerusalem before.

'He who has not seen Jerusalem in its glory has not seen a beautiful city,' said Zechariah.

'It is the city of David where the Holy Ark was taken and where the great King Solomon built the first temple,' another added. The children sat around and listened as the history of their people was retold in the great stories about Abraham, Moses and King David.

The next morning they were up early again before travelling onwards. For several days they walked, stopping only when the heat of the day forced them to rest or as nightfall came. Sometimes they sang the pilgrim hymns which they knew by heart. 'I will lift up my eyes unto the hills,' they sang as they marched along. As they reached the summit of one hill the leaders stopped and pointed. There before them, still some way off, but clearly visible in the sun, was the city of Jerusalem. The white walls sparkled in the sunlight. As the group of travellers stood together they started to sing quietly at first and then the music swelling to a great sound of joy.

'I rejoiced when they said unto me
let us go to the house of the Lord.
Now we stand within thy gates O Jerusalem.
Jerusalem is come to be a city where people come together in unity.
Pray for the peace of Jerusalem.
May those who love you prosper.
For the sake of these my brothers and my friends
I will say "Peace be within you".'

The last note of the psalm died away and Jesus stood with Mary and Joseph gazing towards the city. They were in sight of the city of Jerusalem. Their journey of pilgrimage was almost finished but the Festival of Passover still lay ahead.

MUSIC AND REFLECTION

Introduce the music and ask the children to imagine the journey of Jesus and his family to Jerusalem.

HYMN

He who would valiant be *(Come and Praise No. 44)*

THEME 4: Week 2

SUMMER TERM

PRAYER

We pray for all who are making a pilgrimage today. For those who journey to special places in the hope of finding healing, forgiveness or a new purpose in their life or simply to give thanks for all the good things of life.

May we treat each day as a pilgrimage, a chance to grow closer to our God.

Amen

CLOSING REFRAIN

Shalom *(Come and Praise No. 141)*

TRAVELLING FURTHER

In your worship time try to:

● Foster the idea of pilgrimage as a journey with a special purpose.
● Gain insight into the great places of pilgrimage in the world.
● Explore the idea of life as a pilgrimage whereby we grow in understanding of ourselves, each other and our God.
● Develop the idea of journeys having both good and difficult parts.

Make a pilgrimage game. This is a game rather like 'Snakes and Ladders'. Divide the group into pairs. Each pair will need a piece of card about 30cms square, some counters and a die. On the card draw a curving road about 2.5cms wide. Divide the road into sections about 5cms long. Mark the beginning and end of the journey. Ask the children to devise easy and hard parts of the journey and draw them in some of the sections with a penalty or a reward; e.g. a picture of mountains with the words 'attacked by robbers in the mountains, move back three places. A picture of a pool with trees around it with the words, 'rest by pool, miss a turn'.

Tell the children about John Bunyan's book *The Pilgrim's Progress*.

Find out about great centres of pilgrimage; e.g. Canterbury, Mecca, Benares, Jerusalem.

Tell the children about Chaucer's *Canterbury Tales*. In small groups ask them to prepare a tale to tell each other to entertain the pilgrims.

Read the story of Jesus' first pilgrimage to Jerusalem and find out what happened to him (Luke 2. 41 – 52).

Prepare one of the Pilgrim Psalms (Psalms 120 – 134) to say as a group.

■ SUMMER TERM ■

USEFUL BOOKS

Pilgrimages by Jon Mayled, Religious Topics Series (published by Wayland). *Pilgrimages and Journeys* by Katherine Prior, Understanding Religion Series (published by Wayland).

ON THE HOME STRAIGHT

Collective worship for the end of the week

GATHERING

Remind the children of the theme of pilgrimage.

LISTENING

Ask the children to re-tell one of their pilgrimage stories or to recite a pilgrimage Psalm. Alternatively show slides or a video about a centre of pilgrimage.

MUSIC AND REFLECTION

Introduce the music and ask the children to think about what makes a pilgrimage a special kind of journey.

HYMN

How lovely on the mountains *(Junior praise No. 84)*

PRAYER

Lord God help us as we travel along in our lives.
Give us courage when the way is hard.
Grant us strength when the path is steep and faith when it seems we have lost our way.

Amen

CLOSING REFRAIN

Shalom *(Come and Praise No. 141)*

SUMMER TERM

THEME 4: Week 3

THEME FOR THE WEEK
Journeys of faith

AIM: To familiarize the children with some of the great stories of journeys of faith.

SETTING OUT
Collective worship for the beginning of the week

GATHERING

Remind the children of the theme of journeys and ask the children to suggest the things they would need before setting out; e.g maps, timetables, money for tickets, directions about route, food. Ask the children if they have ever been on a mystery tour and explain that that is one where only the leader knows the destination. Ask if anyone has been on a treasure hunt and explain that that involves following clues to find treasure.

Introduce the story by telling the children that the journey you are going to tell them about was one of mystery and risk, a journey taken without maps and with no idea of the final end.

 LISTENING

This is a story of long, long ago. Long before your parents and grandparents were born, long before Queen Victoria reigned, long before the Romans lived, even before Jesus was born.

The story is about a man called Abraham. He was married to a beautiful wife called Sarah and lived in a city, called Haran, with Abraham's father and his nephew Lot. Haran was on the edge of the desert but because they were near two great rivers the people of Haran could grow crops. There were fine flourishing plantations where the food was plentiful. Haran was a prosperous city. The people who lived there wore rich clothes and jewellery made of gold and silver and precious stones. They lived in fine houses where they made music and listened to poetry.

Abraham was restless. When he was quiet and alone he heard a voice. He thought it was the voice of God but he could hardly believe what God was asking him to do.

But the voice inside him would not be silenced.

'Abraham, leave your own country, your father, friends and neighbours and go to a country which I will show you. I will bless you and make you into a great nation.'

Abraham could hardly believe his ears. Could God really mean him to leave the security of his fine house and the safety of the city? What would his old father think, or his wife? But as Abraham stood at the edge of the city and looked out over the open desert land the voice persisted. Again and again it repeated: 'Abraham, go to a country which I will show you'.

When Abraham shared his thoughts with his friends they were amazed. Some of them even thought Abraham was a little mad. Abraham quietly persisted, deep in his heart he somehow knew that he must obey the inward call. He gathered his flocks and possessions and with Sarah, his wife, and Lot, his nephew, set out on a journey with an unknown destination. It was a journey in which they had to trust their God. A risky journey. A journey of faith.

Adapted from Genesis 12.

 ## MUSIC AND REFLECTION

Introduce the music and ask the children to imagine how Abraham felt as he set out from Haran.

 ## HYMN

Father hear the prayer we offer (*Come and Praise No. 48*)

 ## PRAYER

Lord God, sometimes we have to set out on a journey without knowing its end. Help us to have faith and to trust you to bring us safely to its conclusion.

Amen

 ## CLOSING REFRAIN

Shalom (*Come and Praise No. 141*)

TRAVELLING FURTHER

In your worship time try to:

- Explore and discover examples of journeys undertaken in the spirit of faith.
- Explore how journeys of faith must necessarily entail risk.
- Give the children some chance to experience trust in someone other than themselves.

Play a 'trust journey'. This is a game for pairs. One of the couple is blindfolded and is led by the other on a journey around the room making sure they come to no harm. This could be leading by touch or by verbal instruction. Partners should then reverse roles. Discuss the experience of leading and being lead.

Tell or read the story of Ananias and his journey to Saul (Acts 9. 10 – 19).

Find out about the journey of a great missionary or explorer. Read from the beginning of Chapter 1 to the paragraph ending 'Then he ran' of *I am David* by Anne Holm (published by Mammoth press). Discuss how David set out on his journey.

- Did he need courage?
- When did he have to trust others or himself?

Share the experiences of setting out on a journey when fear has to be overcome and trust or faith are necessary; e.g. a first flight in an aeroplane, visiting a strange place, setting out on a journey alone.

 ## USEFUL BOOKS

The First Men on the Moon by Tim Furness (published by Wayland).
The First Transatlantic Flight by Mike Rosen (published by Wayland).
The First Voyage Around the World by Roger Coote (published by Wayland).
The Voyages of Christopher Columbus by Rupert Matthews (published by Wayland).
The Race to the South Pole by Rupert Matthews (published by Wayland).

======= **SUMMER TERM** =======

ON THE HOME STRAIGHT
Collective worship for the end of the week

This worship session could be used for the final collective worship of the term.

⬇ GATHERING

Remind the children of the theme of journeys. Share some of the stories of journeys they have discovered during the past week. Suggest that they have taken part in a kind of journey through the school year and ask what are the most memorable experiences of that year. These could be of starting with a new class in the Autumn Term, of preparations for Christmas, of outings, Sports Day, concerts or of mastering a new skill. Introduce and read the following story.

LISTENING

TIM MOVES ON

It was the last day of the school term. The morning had been very busy. There was so much to do. The library books had to be collected and put back in the right place. Then there was the sports equipment to check and tidy. The skipping ropes were tied up neatly and the balls put in order. In the classrooms the exercise books were tied in neat bundles ready to be moved to the children's new classes. The desks had been cleared, the pictures taken down from the walls and the displays dismantled. Everywhere looked strangely bare.

In the afternoon there was a film for the whole school to watch and finally there had been a service in the main hall. Now Tim and his friends were in the classroom collecting their coats and bags. It really was the last day of the the Summer term. Tim put on his coat. He felt rather strange. Next year he would be starting at a new school.

'Bye Mr Thompson,' Tim said, as he walked out of the classroom with Matthew his best friend.

'Cheerio Tim. Good bye Matthew and good luck for starting at St Thomas's school next autumn,' replied Mr Thompson.

'Thanks,' the boys answered. They walked slowly down the corridor. Usually they were in a rush to be out and would hurry off home to watch the television or play football in the park. Today it was somehow different. It felt strange to think they would no longer come to this school. They passed the classroom for year one. Miss Baker was still there. Tim stuck his head around the door.

'Bye Miss Baker,' he said. She looked up.

'So you're off now are you?' she smiled.

SUMMER TERM

Tim nodded.

'I can remember your first day at school Tim, do you? You were quite small and couldn't reach the peg to hang up your coat. Quite a change now. You're certainly a big lad now. In fact you could put this paper on the top shelf in my cupboard for me.' Tim stretched up and put the paper away for Miss Baker, who replied, 'Thanks and all the best for the future'.

Tim and Matthew walked on. They passed the hall which was quiet and empty. 'Do you remember playing the recorder in the concert in the fourth year,' Matthew asked.

'Do I! I accidentally knocked the music stand over and we had to start again,' Tim laughed. 'There's an orchestra at our new school. I might try to join it,' reflected Tim. They swung through the doors and out into the playground. 'I shall miss our games of football in the playground,' Tim went on.

'I can't see why we can't still do that at St Thomas's,' said Matthew, 'and there's a really big area for games and sport. Perhaps we could get into a team.' The friends walked through the school gates and turned for one last look.

'You two still hanging around,' called a voice across the playground. 'Time to move on or I'll be asking you back to sort out the computer room.' It was Mr Thompson.

'Come on Matthew. I'll race you to the bus stop,' shouted Tim.

'Not a chance,' laughed Matthew, and they ran off excitedly.

MUSIC AND REFLECTION

Introduce the music and reflect on the story. Is it sad to move on? Were the people in the story looking forward to new things?

HYMN

You shall go out with joy (Come and Praise No. 98)

PRAYER

We give thanks for this last school year.
We give thanks for all the happy times we have enjoyed.
We give thanks for all the skills we have learned.
We give thanks for all the friends we have made.
We give thanks for the opportunities which lie ahead.
We ask for courage and faith to start the next part of our lives trusting God to guide and protect us in all that we do.

Amen

CLOSING REFRAIN

Shalom (Come and Praise No. 141)